EXTREME
DOUBLE-KNITTING

EXTREME DOUBLE-KNITTING

new adventures in reversible colorwork

ALASDAIR POST-QUINN

COOPERATIVE PRESS
Cleveland, OH
cooperativepress.com

ISBN 13: 978-0-9792017-7-6
First Edition
Published by Cooperative Press
http://www.cooperativepress.com

Models: Laura Laa Ceredona, David Dio Trittschuh, Alison Malcolm and Clara Malcolm

FOR COOPERATIVE PRESS

Senior Editor: Shannon Okey
Technical Editor: Andi Smith

THIS BOOK IS DEDICATED TO:

My lovely wife Amanda, who, in our first year of marriage and our first year of homeownership, has put up with my obsession admirably, and with whom I look forward to spending much more social time "now that the book is done."

My good friend and Common Cod Fiber Guild president Guido, whose constant refrain of "How's the book going?" has helped me to keep my priorities straight.

And my cat, Embers, without whose complete disinterest in yarn this book would not have been possible.

TABLE OF CONTENTS

AUTHOR'S NOTE

It's hard to believe that I first started talking about writing a book on double-knitting back in 2006. Five years ago, I had barely scratched the surface of the technique and I was already feeling like there was more about it in my head than was available in printed form. Since then, there have been several other books including double-knitting instructions in some quantity. Double-knitting patterns have become a little more commonplace in books and online. Each time a new book came out that hinted at some element of double-knitting, I hoped/feared that the work I was doing would be published by someone else, freeing me from the obligation to publish it myself. But in these past 5 years, it became clear that it was going to be up to me to make sure that the full breadth of double-knitting was given the exposure it deserves.

I struggled for a while, deciding what direction to steer this book. Originally, the concept was a sort of encyclopedia of everything that was possible to do using the technique, from the mundane to the truly bizarre. I considered double-knitting such a niche technique, and thought that an encyclopedia of it wouldn't actually be all that big of a project. Boy, was I wrong.

It's 2011 now, and I've settled comfortably into a sub-niche of double-knitting, specifically dealing with colorwork. I've barely done any tubular double-knitting at all. That technique will be mentioned here and there in this text, and given a section in the appendix, but it's not where I've focused my time and gained my expertise. I've experimented with textured double-knitting, and even simple two-sided openwork. It was a worthwhile experiment that gave me a better understanding of the fabric's structure, but I kept coming back to color.

I love color. I love geometric designs and the interplay of colorways. But I am also very utilitarian-minded — I don't like wasted space. As a younger man, I became an accomplished paper-folder, and was well-known in origami circles, even if I never achieved my dream of becoming a well-known designer. I did counted cross-stitch and Chinese knotwork. In college, I was an art major, focusing on sculpture. I have always had a keen eye for the underlying structure of things, and how they fit together. I suppose it's not surprising I embraced knitting when I learned it, even as late in life as I did. I was designing my own knitted objects almost right off the bat — I was obsessed with Möbius scarves. At some point, I stumbled across a copy of Jane Neighbors' book in my local library, and began to play with double-knitting — and it was all downhill from there. Ironically, I never did make a double-knit Möbius scarf, but there's still time, right?

I chose to write this book as a compendium of double-knitting colorwork techniques, as in-depth as I could make it, to help other people really understand double-knitting at a fundamental level. But as I worked, I began to discover techniques that I couldn't find any documentation for at all, and had to begin to think of my own terminology and my own ways for charting and describing them. Even now, I am aware that this book is merely a snapshot of my current repertoire of double-knitting techniques. I am still thinking about further refinements and techniques, and I'm hoping that this book will get other people thinking about what else could be possible when knitting is not limited to a single face. Perhaps you will have seen the same techniques described or done differently in other books; perhaps you will immediately see an easier way to do something.

If I can get your mind working in a new and different way, I consider that a success.

Alasdair Post-Quinn

INTRODUCTION

WHAT IS DOUBLE-KNITTING?

From as early as the 19th century, and perhaps earlier, double-knitting has been practiced in Europe. As knitting developed in isolated communities around the globe, the term "double knitting" (as opposed to "double-knitting") came to mean several things. Around the world today, double knitting or DK is a weight of yarn, the term referring to the thickness. In Nova Scotia, double knitting is merely a term for any two-color stranded knitting. People confuse the name with doubling — the practice of knitting your yarn doubled when you want a higher gauge in a particular fiber.

But double-knitting — the technique to which this book is dedicated — is not known by any other names that I have heard. In the most basic sense, it is the technique of hand-knitting two fabrics at once on the same set of needles.

I imagine the long-forgotten originator of this technique sitting by the fireside, holding a 1x1 ribbed scarf and idly pulling the fabric in one direction to separate the ribs, then in the other direction to recompress them. She looked it over on both sides and noticed that the compressed fabric strongly resembled stockinette stitch on both sides, to the point that she could imagine it as two independent fabrics lying back to back. She picked up her needles, pulled two ends from the basket of yarn at her side, and cast on. But this time, rather than ribbing, she held the ends together, and worked the knits in one color and the purls in the other. Thus, I imagine, double-knitting was born.

At its most basic, it really is that simple. The two sides of the fabric are actually separate, unless they are joined in some way during the work. Double-knitting can be worked in one color or two — or, as you will see later, in three or more colors. In one color, the most often-used technique is tubular double-knitting, in which you slip every other stitch to create a tubular fabric such as a sleeve or a sock on a single set of needles. In multiple colors, you have the option to do reversible colorwork motifs which hold the two sides of that tubular fabric together. In this way, the technique goes from a novel way to knit a normal garment to a unique addition to your repertoire that makes a fabric that can't be created in any other way.

WHAT IS DOUBLE-KNITTING GOOD FOR & WHY WOULD YOU DO IT?

With the techniques laid out in this book, you'll come to realize that almost any plain or colorworked garment can, with some adaptation, be converted to double-knitting simply by translating the single-sided instructions to a double-sided method for doing the same thing. However, just because you can do it doesn't mean you should. Double-knitting is time-consuming and impractical for some garments — if all you want is a double thickness for extra warmth, there are other ways to do that. The types of patterns that benefit most from double-knitting are the ones that can make visual use of the reversibility. These include washcloths, potholders, scarves, headbands, hats, neckties, and on up to vests, cardigans, handbags, and blankets of all sizes; you can also use elements of the technique to create cushions, button bands, collars, cuffs, and even pockets. I'm sure you'll find your own creative uses for it as well.

Of course, tubular double-knitting (a technique well covered by Beverly Royce and not fully documented here) is good for socks, mittens, gloves, sleeves, and anything else you'd normally have to knit on several DPNs.

I've been asked a number of times about the benefit of double-knitting something rather than doing two separate pieces and stitching them together. It seems that "because you can" isn't a good enough answer for most people — nor should it be.

When people ask me this, I usually bring up the example of the so-called "sausage hat". Even if the name doesn't ring a bell, you've probably seen what I mean — two hats seamed together at the brim so that one can be turned inside out and stuffed inside the other. Anyone who's worn one of these can probably attest to the fact that the inside layer is always a little bunchy and takes some adjusting before it's comfortable. Because both layers are completely separate except where they attach at the brim and possibly at the crown, they tend to slide out of alignment with each other and are generally a bit messy. Sure, they're warm, they're simple, and if that's all you're going for they're probably fine.

But me, I'm going for something a little more than that. I like a double-thick hat that's worked as a single fabric, that doesn't bunch up inside because the two layers are anchored together, and that looks equally good worn either side out. I like working both sides at the same time because I know both sides will be the same size. I like the freedom of being able to do colorwork anywhere I want without worrying about stranding or twisting. I hope you'll find your own reasons to love double-knitting as well.

WHAT CAN I EXPECT FROM THIS BOOK?

I thought long and hard about what I wanted to include in this book. Originally, the idea was to make an encyclopedia of everything that could possibly be done in double-knitting. However, my true interest is in colorwork, so I will leave the instructions on tubular double-knitting and textured double-knitting to others who can devote time to that research.

This book is meant to teach knitters (people who already know how to knit) a technique and variations on that technique. With each new variation, your options are expanded and I'll present a new pattern or two. By the time you have learned all the techniques and variations, you will have the repertoire needed to handle the final pattern. The patterns themselves are generally small objects and garments that won't take months to do, but will give you the practice you need to master each new technique. Once you have mastered them, you may choose to apply your new-found knowledge to larger constructions. I will look forward to seeing what you do with your new knowledge!

That said, this book is not for the person who's never taken up yarn and needles before. There are plenty of books that will teach you how to knit. Once you know how to knit and purl, however, most of the techniques in this book will be open to you.

CHAPTER 1: THE BASICS

THE STRUCTURE OF DOUBLE-KNIT FABRIC

Double-knit fabric is comprised of two layers, worked simultaneously. In reality, you are knitting a layer of stockinette with a layer of reverse stockinette behind it. The end result is a fabric that appears to have no wrong side — the stockinette faces outward, while the purl sides of both layers face each other inside the work. If each side is a separate solid color, then the fabric is hollow — you can pinch each side and separate it. If you wanted, you could separate the layers before binding off and stuff it with batting. However, if you change colors within a row, the two sides will lock together.

All double-knitting is worked in pairs of stitches. If something happens to the stitch on the facing side of the pair, something has to happen to the one on the opposite side as well. Depending on the technique you're using, the opposite side can be worked at (nearly) the same time as the facing side, or using a second pass to complete a row or round.

When color changes are included, you have the freedom to create motif patterns, all-over patterns, lettering — really, anything that can be charted. Any time a color is used on one side, its opposite color is used on the other side. This means a number of things. First, it means that any two-color design can be double-knitted without worry about strand length. Likewise, any amount of space can be put between motifs without worrying about wasting yarn. If it weren't for the double thickness, we would have just put Fair Isle and intarsia out of business. It also means that motifs that are asymmetrical will show up in mirror image on the opposite side.

While it may seem that the two sides are precise mirror images of one another, they are actually positioned one half-pair off from each other. This makes logical sense since the stitches on the needle alternate between facing and opposite sides. However, large expanses of color with no color changes (which I call plain double-stockinette) will tend to shift so that the stitches match their opposite numbers on the other side. Once color changes are integrated into the fabric, the half-pair offset becomes more pronounced. Still, to the untrained eye the fabric is perfectly reversible.

WORKING WITH DOUBLE-KNITTING GAUGE

When I first started double-knitting, I was astounded to find out that the stitches I was making were very nearly square. This made graphing my first charts very easy — normal graph paper was sufficient. As I've progressed further, perhaps my tension has relaxed a bit. My stitches aren't quite square anymore, but they're still not as oblong as I understand most knitters' stitches are.

In all my reading of others' double-knitting instructions, I have heard a staggering number of personal experiences presented as absolute facts. People will say that double-knitting stitches are slightly looser, slightly tighter, that you can get away with using the same needles as usual for a given yarn in single-faced knitting, or that you absolutely must go down several needle sizes to achieve anything close to the correct gauge. These are all wrong.

There is only one fact when it comes to gauge: everyone's is different. Case in point: I have a friend who needs to use US2 needles to get the same gauge in double-knitting that I get with US6.

You cannot get away from gauge swatching in double-knitting. Unless you are well experienced with a particular yarn using a particular size of needles in double-knitting, you will need to make a gauge swatch. It doesn't have to be huge. It doesn't even have to be 4" across. At bare minimum, it needs to have enough stitches so you can determine how many stitches fit in an inch, to the nearest half stitch. At 4", you can be even more precise by dividing by 4.

It's also important that the fabric you are swatching with bears as much resemblance to the fabric in the final piece you are swatching for as possible. Various things can affect your gauge: whether you are knitting flat or in the round; whether your fabric is heavily patterned or largely plain double-stockinette, whether your stitches are twisted or not; and of course the thickness of your yarn and the size of your needles.

When working in the round, your gauge on the facing and opposite side may be different. Most people's knit and purl gauges are slightly different — and when double-knitting in the round, all of the stitches on the facing side are knits, and all the stitches on the opposite side are purls. The most common outcome of this is for the opposite side to be slightly larger than the facing side. This is awkward in a final garment because the opposite side is worn inside at least half the time, and if the inside layer is bulkier than the outside, it tends to be obvious. However, the effect can be minimized simply by turning the final piece inside out. The effect is also minimized if the pattern includes plenty of color changes — since the two sides are locked together where the colors change, the two gauges help each other average out. The discrepancy between facing and opposite-side gauges will fix itself with practice — in the meantime, you should use the larger gauge (smaller number of stitches per inch) to determine the size. The other side will stretch to accommodate — as long as you're only off by a stitch per inch at most.

In order to take accurate gauge measurements in the round, you really should do a gauge swatch in the round. You can choose to either do a small tube on DPNs or your preferred small-diameter technique, or you can do a small flat piece but instead of turning and going back on an opposite side row, extend the active ends around the back of the piece and then start in again on the facing side. Make sure the hanging loops are loose enough so that the resulting fabric can lie flat.

When working in flat double-knitting, however, the knit and purl sides alternate. On facing-side rows, the facing side is knit and the opposite side is purled; on opposite-side rows, the opposite side faces you and is knit, while the facing side is purled. If your knit and purl gauges are significantly off, you may notice horizontal ridges as the rows alternate looser and tighter. This too will fix itself with practice; in the meantime, it is usually safe to take gauge measurements since both sides of the fabric should end up with the same gauge.

In a pinch, you can use a flat double-knit swatch to figure a rough gauge for a piece done in the round — because the two sides' gauges average out, the measurement will be similar to the average of the two sides done separately in the round. It won't be a precise measurement, but I understand if you're in a hurry — just as long as you don't expect perfection.

DOUBLE-KNITTING TERMINOLOGY

Double-knitting isn't yet a truly mainstream knitting technique. There are numerous knitters who have their own terminology for double-knitting techniques and variations, but little standard vocabulary in common use by all knitters. Because of this, I will risk confusing the issue by using the terminology I have always used in my workshops and patterns. I don't expect my vocabulary to be added wholesale to the global knitting lexicon, but I hope that the way I describe my work will be understandable and that you will be able to use my vocabulary to explain your work in the future.

I have had to come up with names for a few techniques I have not seen before (for example, 2K2 or lock knit — see page 135). It is possible that these moves have other names. I am willing to adopt these other names in the future if they're more elegant than what I came up with, but since they're fairly specialized I don't anticipate much argument from the community.

I prefer to refer to the primary technique as "double-knitting" and to the fabric as "double-knit". The hyphen is there to acknowledge that the two words go together to make a concrete term, and that if separated they can mean other things.

For the purpose of this book, I am avoiding the accepted terminology of "MC" and "CC" for main color and contrasting color respectively. This is because these terms are useful only as long as you're working with two colors. Once you add a third or fourth color (or beyond), two color designations are inadequate. Instead, the patterns will use "Color A" through "Color D" and other areas where MC and CC would be used will use more interchangeable terminology as well.

The term "wrong side" is also a bit of a misnomer in double-knitting, since the whole point of the technique is to make a fabric with two right sides and no wrong side. For this reason, I will try to keep from using "right" and "wrong" or "front" and "back", in favor of "facing" and "opposite" for the two sides, and simply "knit" and "purl" for the elements of each pair.

Finally, I call the colored elements of my charts "pixels" — probably because I come from a computer background. A pixel is an individual element of color on a computer display. It's usually square. The reason you don't see pixels in general is because they're very tiny and most displays allow them to be any one of around 16 million colors, whereas in my charts they're much larger and generally only one of 2 to 4 colors. But they're the same thing — an element in a grid, used to simulate a picture by changing colors.

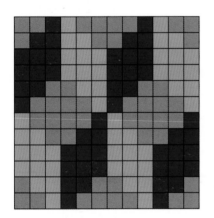 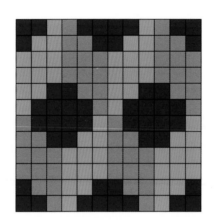 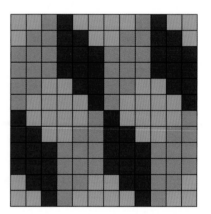

Each "pixel" represents one colored stitch.

IN DEFENSE OF TWISTED STITCHES

I am a self-taught knitter. Well, someone taught me how to do my first knit stitches, and I made a tiny garter-stitch square. But then I taught myself to purl from a book, and enveloped myself in the knowledge of knitting techniques while sitting in my dorm room at college. At that point I knew few knitters. I visited my local yarn shop and bought chunky yarn and large needles. I hung out at the knitting group that met there periodically, and I grew as a knitter. But nobody scrutinized my knitting, and in reality I was just strengthening my own "bad" habit — I had taught myself to knit my stitches twisted.

When I branched out and visited another local yarn shop a bit further from my home base, the proprietor took one look at my work and said, "You're doing it wrong!" I was mortified. Upon closer inspection of my own knitting and someone else's work, it became clear that my stitches had a distinct "braided" look whereas the norm appeared to be stitches that have a split down the middle.

But I was already well into the pattern and I didn't feel like changing it. I kept twisting my stitches. I liked the way it looked, and still do.

At some point, I realized how I was creating twisted stitches, and I realized how easily I could create untwisted stitches. However, rather than breathing a sigh of relief and changing my ways, I simply realized I had more control over my knitting than I had previously. I kept doing twisted stitches in my early double-knitting work — but I used untwisted stitches for openwork or other people's patterns. I didn't do many patterns by other people. I had been designing my own garments since day one, essentially.

But why did I keep doing the twisted stitches? When I first started, I was a very tight knitter. I still am, but I've relaxed somewhat. Twisted stitches were almost perfectly square. This meant that a chart done on standard graph paper came out quite close to the chart when knitted. As my gauge has changed over the years, that is less true but still close enough that only minor blocking is necessary to achieve square-ness again.

In truth, my untwisted gauge is not that far off from square either. But as I experimented with both, I realized another reason to use twisted stitches. Double-knitting is done in two layers, and the facing layer is almost always a different color from the opposite layer. If you pull laterally on double-knit fabric, the fabric expands by inserting space between the stitches. If the stitches are untwisted, they also split in half. This means that not only do the colored stitches lose their definition; they also expose the color of the opposite side more thoroughly. Twisted stitches, on the other hand, don't lose their definition (pulling on them doesn't split them in half) and the only portions that expose the opposite side are the spaces between the stitches.

However, this is a personal choice. Some people will like the look of twisted stitches and be willing to learn a new way to knit; some people will prefer to stay with tradition and what they know. If there's one thing I learned many years ago, it's that you never say "You're doing it wrong" to a knitter. If you're happy with the result, you're doing it just right.

CHAPTER 2: DOUBLE-KNITTING FLAT AND IN THE ROUND

STANDARD DOUBLE-KNITTING CAST-ON

In general, even if your pattern is for more than two colors, your cast-on will use only two colors — typically the background colors from the two sides. So that the cast-on instructions are universal — i.e. they can be applied to any pattern in this book, whether done flat or in the round — we will refer to the two colors not as the well-known MC and CC, but as TC (thumb color) and FC (finger color).

The cast-on is based on the long-tail method I learned from my mother — but there is no long tail. Instead, you will be using the long-tail techniques on the active ends. The nice thing about this is that you get the clean edge usually associated with the long-tail cast-on without all the tedious guesswork.

To begin, make a slip-knot with both colors held together, insert the needle through the loop and tighten. Leave about a 4-6" tail for weaving in. Don't worry about which direction the slip-knot colors are facing — you will remove and untie the knot after you complete your first row or before you start your first round.

between the two hanging active ends. The color hanging over your thumb will be called TC (thumb color) and the color hanging over your finger will be called FC (finger color).

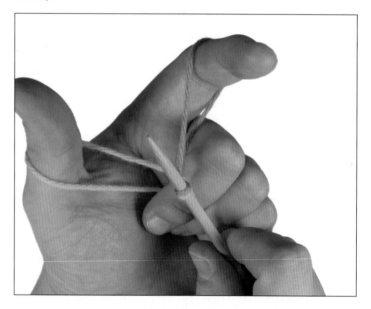

2) Close the rest of your fingers over the hanging ends; spread your thumb and forefinger into a Y-shape, and pull the needle back like a slingshot. The ends should come from the needle, pass through the middle of the Y, around each finger from the inside to the outside, and continue down into your closed hand, out the bottom of your loosely-held fist, and into your wound source balls.

You will need to differentiate among the four end segments for the next several steps. From the front to the back, you should have the outer TC, the inner TC, the inner FC and the outer FC.

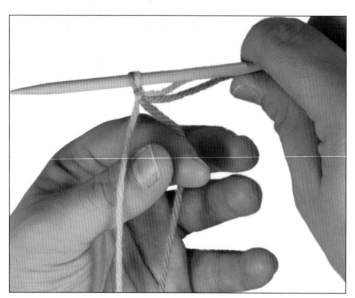

1) Position your hands. With the needle in your right hand and the tails held out of the way in that hand, put your left forefinger and thumb together and put them

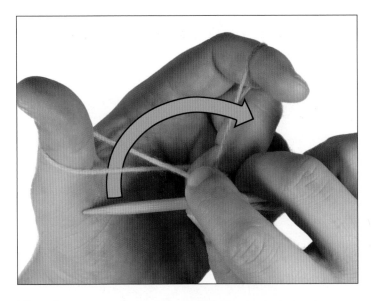

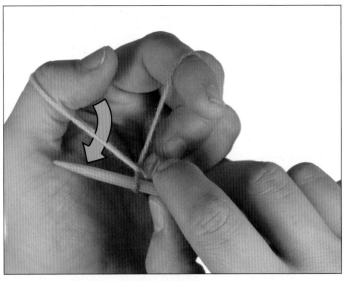

3) With your needle in front of all the ends, bring it up underneath the outer TC. Pass the needle over the top of both inner TC and inner FC ...

5) Drop the thumb loop, pick up the hanging end of TC on your thumb again, and tighten. You should have a loop of FC on your needle.

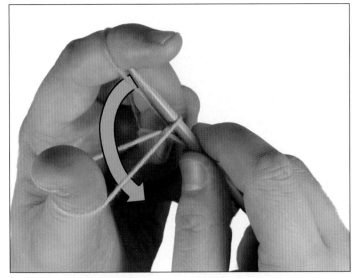

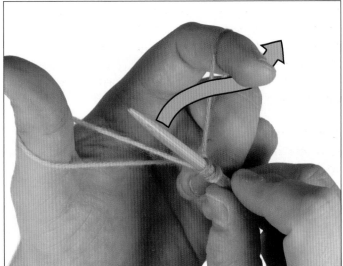

4) ... then down between the inner FC and outer FC. Pull the inner FC down with the needle tip; with that loop of FC on your needle, pass the needle back down between the inner and outer TC ends (the same way you came in).

6) Next, we'll do the same thing in mirror image for a reverse long-tail cast-on stitch. Bring your needle in back of all of the ends.

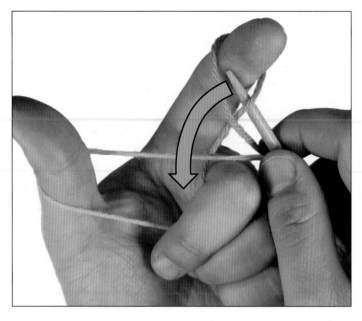

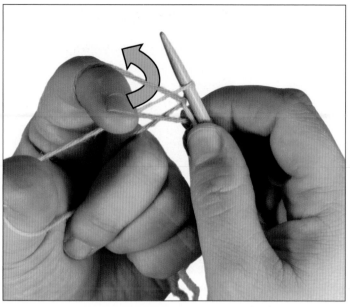

7) Bring your needle up from underneath the outer FC. Pass the needle over the top of both inner FC and TC, then down in between the inner and outer TC.

9) Drop the finger loop, pick up the hanging end of FC on your finger again, and tighten.

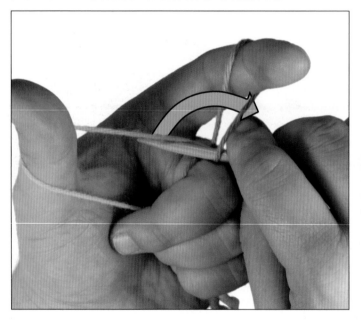

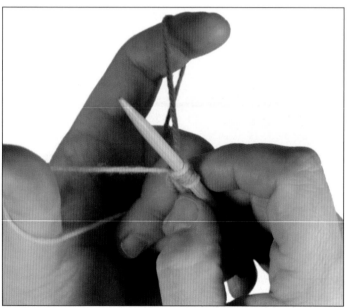

8) Pull the inner TC up with the needle tip; with that loop of TC on your needle, pass the needle back up between the inner and outer FC ends (the same way you came in).

10) This has created a pair of stitches, the first in your FC and the second in your TC. Continue doing one regular and one reverse long-tail cast-on stitch to continue alternating cast-on colors. I recommend you tighten this cast-on a little more than you normally would for a long-tail cast-on. It will make the first row after the cast-on more difficult, but the final edge will be much cleaner.

DOUBLE-KNITTING STITCHES

These are the rules of standard double-knitting:

All double-knitting is worked in pairs. The first stitch in the pair is always the facing-side stitch, is always knit, and is always worked with all active ends in back (wyib). The second stitch in the pair is always the opposite-side stitch, is always purled, is always worked with all active ends in front (wyif), AND is always worked in the opposite color from the facing-side stitch.

In truth, they're little more than guidelines, and as the book goes on we'll break a few of them, but they are the foundation on which the structure of double-knitting is built.

As I mentioned earlier, I like the look of twisted stitches in double-knitting. Most people twist their stitches by knitting or purling into the back loop. I don't, and I think my method is more efficient — and translates more smoothly into other knitting techniques. I came up with an amusing pair of names for my style of twisted knitting as compared to the style of untwisted knitting most people practice.

EXTROVERTED DOUBLE-KNITTING

(turning your yarn away from you: all stitches untwisted)

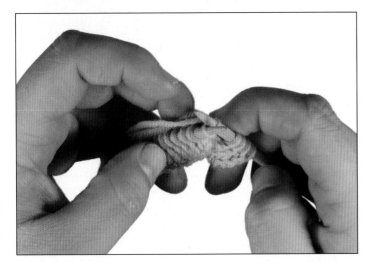

1) With both ends in back, insert your right needle into the left loop as if to knit (in the same orientation as the left needle, and underneath it, pointing from front to back)

2) Wrap the end of the color you need around the needle away from you. If you are looking at the needle point-on, this would be a counter-clockwise wrap. Finish the untwisted knit stitch.

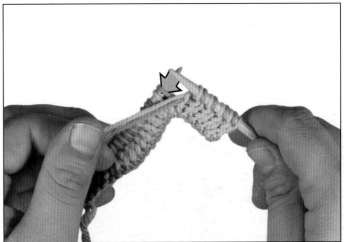

3) With both ends in front, insert your right needle into the next left loop as if to purl (in the opposite orientation from the left needle, and underneath it, pointing from back to front).

4) Wrap the end of the opposite color from the previous stitch around the needle away from you. Finish the untwisted purl stitch.

INTROVERTED DOUBLE-KNITTING

(turning your yarn toward you: all stitches twisted)

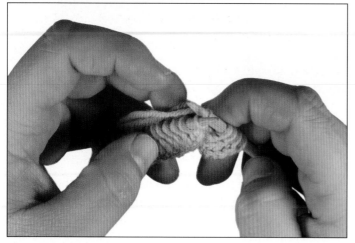

1) With both ends in back, insert your right needle into the left loop as if to knit (in the same orientation as the left needle, and underneath it, pointing from front to back)

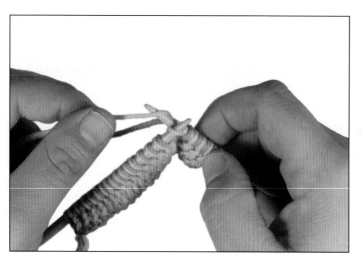

2) Wrap the end of the color you need around the needle toward you. If you are looking at the needle point-on, this would be a clockwise wrap. Finish the twisted knit stitch.

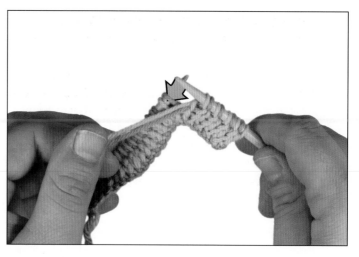

3) With both ends in front, insert your right needle into the next left loop as if to purl (in the opposite orientation from the left needle, and underneath it, pointing from back to front.

4) Wrap the end of the opposite color from the previous stitch around the needle toward you. Finish the twisted purl stitch.

As you can see, the only difference between the two styles is the direction the yarn is wrapped. This may be difficult to translate to your own style of knitting — there are so many — but with practice I firmly believe anyone can get it. Each of the stitch techniques' end results (later in the book) will be shown with both twisted and untwisted stitches to help you choose the look you prefer.

STANDARD ("TWO-COLORS-AT-ONCE") DOUBLE-KNITTING

I never came up with a more elegant name for this technique than the "two-colors-at-once" method, but since it is now considered the standard method of double-knitting, there is no more need to differentiate it from the other method outlined in the Appendix which uses one color at a time. From now on, it will be called simply "standard double-knitting".

STANDARD FLAT DOUBLE-KNITTING

There are two primary ways to achieve flat double-knitting. All of the patterns in this book use the standard method, but the slip-stitch method is described in the Appendix (see page 177)

The flat version of standard double-knitting is worked back and forth in the same way as standard single-faced knitting, so it can be done on any needle you are comfortable with — straight, circular, or double pointed.

STANDARD FLAT DOUBLE-KNITTING CAST-ON

In flat double-knitting, your cast-on will be equivalent to an opposite-side row. Because of this, your colors will be cast-on in reverse order so that when you turn to work your first row, your colors will be properly orientated. Assuming your background color on the facing side is Color A and the background color on the opposite side is Color B, and referring to the cast-on instructions on page 16, make Color A your TC and Color B your FC. This way, the first stitch on the needle will be Color B and the second will be Color A — and when you turn the needle to start the row, the knit stitches will all be Color A and the purl stitches will all be Color B.

WORKING IN STANDARD FLAT DOUBLE-KNITTING

Referring to the rules of double-knitting on page 19, you will be holding both ends together, and knitting only the color required by the stitch you are working. Continuing from the cast-on example above, and assuming you have some plain background in your chart before any color changes are made, your first row will consist of pairs worked thus:

1) Wyib, K1 Color A
2) Wyif, P1 Color B

When you get to the end of your row and turn, you will be working with the opposite side facing you and the facing side away from you — and you will work it like this:

1) Wyib, K1 Color B
2) Wyif, P1 Color A

As you can see, your pair structure doesn't change — the first stitch is always knit, the second always purled — but the colors change because you are working on the opposite side.

When you get to the end of your first row, you can remove and untie the slip-knot. If you are using DPNs or circular needles, you can do this at any time before the end of the first row as well.

STANDARD FLAT DOUBLE-KNITTING EDGES

Edges in flat double-knitting are the bane of many double-knitters' existence. No matter what method you choose, it will probably require long practice before the tension is perfect. There are three edges I use in this book, all with their pros and cons.

CLOSED DOUBLE-KNIT EDGE

This edge is conceptually the simplest, but probably the hardest to pull off cleanly. It is most useful when the pattern needs to go all the way to the edge, but it's very hard to get the tension correct. Even after all my years of double-knitting, I can't get it perfect 100% of the time. It's also useful in certain situations where increases are used (you'll find it at the bottom of Silk City, one of my neckties). It does not require any extra pairs to achieve.

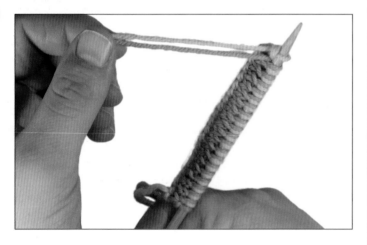

1) At the beginning of your row, note that the first pair has two ends extending from it, and that those ends are separated by a small amount of space. If that space isn't closed up at the beginning of each row, the edge will remain open.

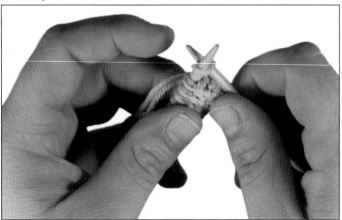

2) With both ends in back, insert your needle into the first stitch of the first pair as if to knit.

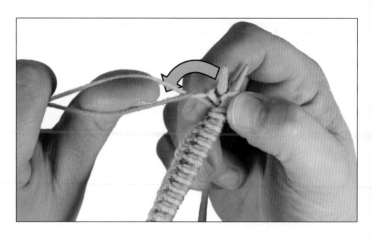

3) Twist the active ends around each other at least 180 degrees — but not more than 360 degrees — to ensure there is a twist between the last pair in the previous row and the first pair in the new row. If you are changing colors between the last pair in the previous row and the first pair in the new row, you don't need to make a conscious effort to twist — the color change itself will lock the edge together.

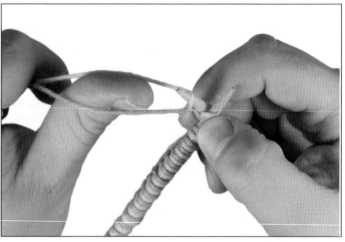

4) Complete the knit stitch with the color required according to the chart.

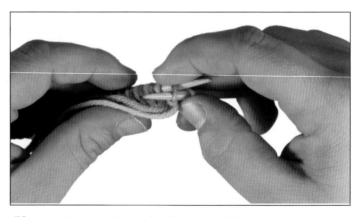

5) Bring both ends to the front. Purl the second stitch in the pair with the opposite color, making sure that the twist is intact. Both ends should be secure if you pull on them.

CLOSED DOUBLE-KNIT SELVEDGE

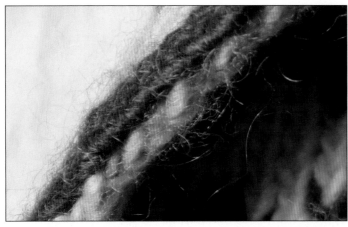

This is, in my opinion, the cleanest possible double-knit edge, and the easiest to achieve. If there is no pressing reason to use any other edge, this is the one you should use. It does require an extra pair on each edge, and has its own chart notation symbol (see the global key, page 188). It may seem like this edge is more work than the non-selvedge method above, but it's really because it incorporates the preparation of the previous row. The ends are twisted in the same way, but because they're integrated into a selvedge, the twists hide inside the edge more readily, and the extra yarn of the selvedge evens up the slack and tension of the column next to it, so it's easier to keep the edge clean.

Work your row to the end of the charted pattern. This should leave one pair on the left needle.

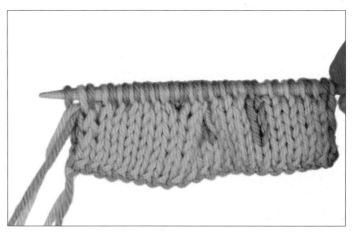

2) Bring both ends to the front; slip 1 stitch purlwise.

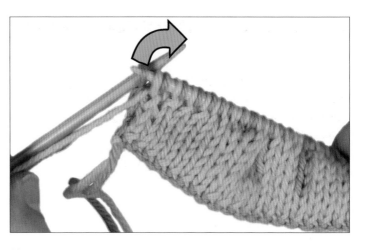

3) At this point, you can turn your work and start the row with a twist (follow Edge Twist steps 1-5).

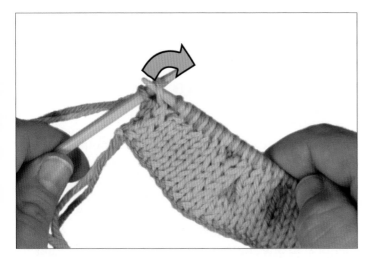

1) With both ends in back, slip 1 stitch purlwise.

OPEN DOUBLE-KNIT EDGE

This method is very specialized and is only used in one pattern in this book (Open for Business, page 99). It's theoretically very easy — since it is achieved simply by not doing something rather than doing something extra — but once you are used to sealing your edges together, it may be more difficult to remember not to. It does have a chart notation symbol (see the global key, page 188).

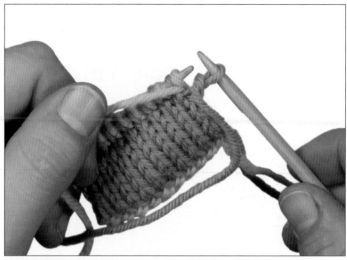

3) Bring both ends to the front. Notice that the facing-side color and the opposite-side color ends are not interlinked.

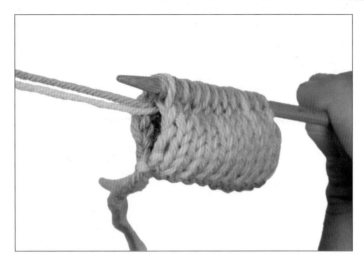

1) This is the end of a row, having just slipped the last pair as in the selvedge section. You can choose to work this technique without a selvedge if you prefer, by working rather than slipping the last pair. Note that the edge of the work is visibly open down to the cast-on edge.

4) Continue with a purl stitch in the opposite-side color. Finish the row as indicated in the pattern.

STANDARD DOUBLE-KNITTING BIND-OFF

There are countless ways to bind off your double-knitting. I am not overly concerned about making the cast-on and bind-off edge look identical, but there are certainly ways to do that if you do enough research and experimentation. In my opinion, it's better to make sure the edges look good and are stable than that they look identical to one another. This is something only other knitters ever notice.

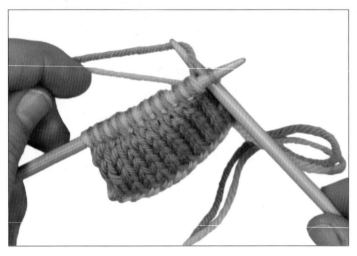

2) Turn and make a knit stitch as normal, with both ends in back, being careful to keep the opposite-side color out of the way.

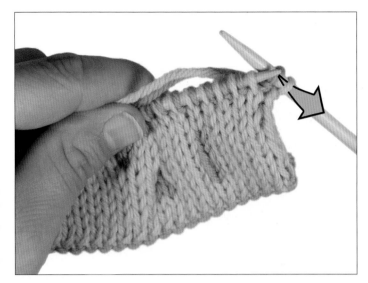

1) Work the first pair in standard double-knitting. You can choose to keep the same colors as the pair below or change them, but you will be using pairs of the same color configuration all the way across — so choose wisely. Insert the left needle tip into the rightmost of the two stitches on your right needle.

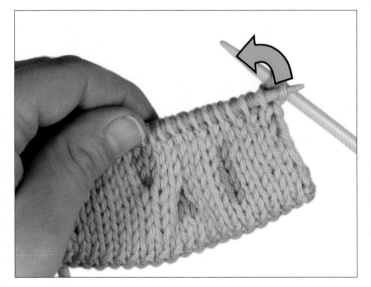

2) Pull the second stitch over the first stitch and off the needle. This is the "normal" technique associated with binding off, called a PSSO (pass second stitch over). You may want to tighten the end corresponding to the color of the loop you just slipped off — but not too much, if a flexible edge is something you value.

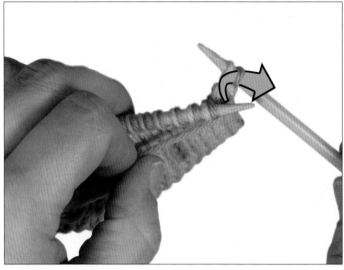

3) With both ends in back, K1 with the same color as the knit stitch in the first pair. Insert the left needle tip into the rightmost of the two stitches on the right needle.

4) Pull the second stitch over the first and off the needle.

5) With both ends in front, P1 with same color as the purl stitch in the first pair

6) PSSO

7) Repeat 3-6 until you have one loop left on the left needle. Pull it out a bit, break both ends and pull them through the last loop. Remove the needle and tighten.

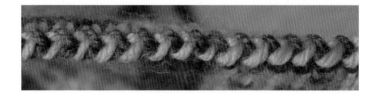

DECORATIVE DOUBLE-KNITTING BIND-OFF

This bind-off is beautiful — but almost completely inflexibility. It's best used for edges that don't need flexibility, but will be prominently visible. I don't recommend it for wearable garments unless the edge is not meant to expand or contract at all. It also bears no resemblance whatsoever to any cast-on I have been able to reproduce, and certainly none to any in this book.

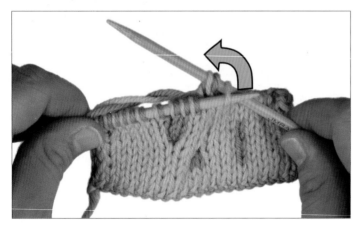

1) Work the first pair in standard double-knitting. You can choose to keep the same colors as the pair below or change them, but you will be using pairs of the same color configuration all the way across so choose wisely.

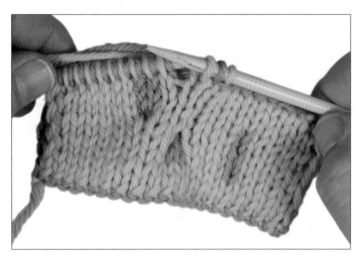

2) With both ends in back, K1 with the same color as the knit stitch in the first pair.

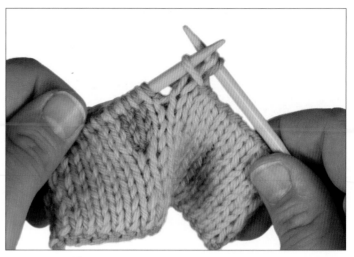

3) Using the left needle tip, pick up the rightmost of the three stitches on your right needle. Pull it over the other two stitches and off the needle. I call this a PTSO (pass third stitch over). You may want to tighten the stitches by pulling on the ends a little as you go to give the bind-off a nice clean definition.

4) With both ends in front, P1 with the same color as the purl stitch in the first pair.

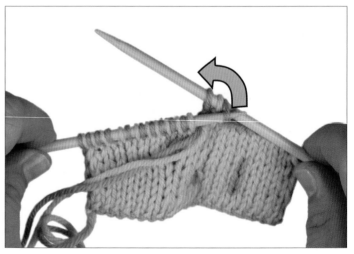

5) Using the left needle tip, pick up the rightmost of the three stitches on your right needle. Pull it over the other two stitches and off the needle.

6) Repeat steps 2-5 until you have 2 loops left on the left needle. Pull them both out a bit, then pass both ends through both loops, remove the needle and tighten.

DOUBLE-KNITTING IN THE ROUND

To a certain degree, double-knitting in the round is simpler than flat double-knitting. The reasons for this are approximately the same reasons why the same is true for single-faced knitting. Ironically, most people start with flat knitting; similarly, most people start double-knitting with a potholder or a coaster, or perhaps a scarf.

In double-knitting as in single-faced knitting, working in the round removes two major trouble spots:

1) Edges. You saw how much time I spent describing edge techniques on pages 22-25. We can skip that whole discussion for double-knitting in the round. There are no edges when you never change direction.

2) Opposite-side rows. In flat double-knitting, the opposite-side row is reversed in color and orientation from the facing-side row, and it isn't generally presented in the pattern. You have to rely on your brain to make the proper translation. In the round, the facing side is always facing you, so there are no opposite-side rows.

In addition, bind-offs are more rare. The majority of pieces done in the round are hats, although mittens, gloves and top-down socks also benefit from the lack of a bind-off.

In trade for the removal of these issues, double-knitting in the round doesn't get off scot-free. Because the opposite side is always done as a series of purls, it runs the risk of having a different gauge from the facing side. In flat double-knitting, every time you turn the work you are changing which side is worked in stockinette and which is done in reverse-stockinette. If you have a difference in your gauge for the two types of fabric, flat double-knitting may even it out for you. In the round, you have to be more careful. See the section on double-knitting gauge, page 12.

Also like single-faced knitting, you will have to use a needle or needle set that can accommodate working in the round — a circular needle is favorite, but double-pointed needles (DPNs) will work for smaller-diameter work, and if you so choose you can use Magic Loop (see instructions in Bev Galeskas' "The Magic Loop" booklet or in countless places on the internet) or the two-circulars method (see instructions on page 136, or more in-depth in Cat Bordhi's "Socks Soar …" booklet)

DOUBLE-KNITTING CAST-ON IN THE ROUND

In double-knitting in the round, your cast-on will be equivalent to a facing-side row. You will be starting your knitting on the same pair that started your cast-on. Therefore, assuming your background color on the facing side is Color A and the background color on the opposite side is Color B, and referring to the cast-on instructions on page 16, make Color A your FC and Color B your TC.

WORKING DOUBLE-KNITTING IN THE ROUND

Double-knitting in the round is done in the same way as flat double-knitting, except that you never need to work an opposite-side row. Once the cast-on is done, you will need to remove and untie the slip-knot at the beginning of the cast-on. Join the two ends, being careful not to twist the cast-on edge, and begin working the pairs according to your chart. When I say to join the ends, I mean it literally. Just bring them together and start knitting where the cast-on started. In standard knitting it is sometimes advisable to switch the first and last stitches before starting knitting, which diminishes the effect of the jog on the cast-on edge, but double-knitting's increased thickness makes this impractical.

STANDARD DOUBLE-KNITTING COLOR-CHANGING

Color changing in double-knitting is done the same way regardless of whether you are working flat or in the round. When a color change is made, the color used on the opposite side is brought forward and used on the facing side; at the same time the color used on the facing side crosses to the opposite side and is used to make the complementary stitch in the pair. When the color is changed back, the ends cross again and return to their original places. Because the strands travel from facing to opposite sides and vice versa, the two layers are locked together any time a color change is made in a row. Color changes between rows do not lock together

— for example, you could have a horizontally-striped flat piece, and as long as the only color change is at the edges, the piece would still be hollow inside. But if the stripes were made vertically, the piece would be locked together and only the vertical stripes would be hollow.

Since you have already done pairs in both configurations while working on the odd and even rows in standard flat double-knitting (see page 21), color-changing should come relatively easily. Again, the rules still apply — the first stitch in each pair is knit and the second is purled — but the colors change, this time not because you're working on the opposite side, but because you want to change colors. If the background pairs are worked (A, B), then a color-changed pair is worked (B, A). The same is of course true in reverse — if the background pairs are worked (B, A), a color-changed pair is worked (A, B).

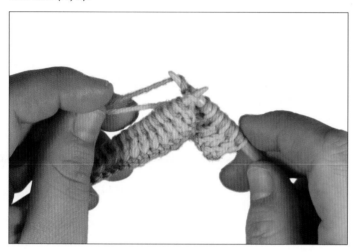

1) Note that the end you are using to make the first stitch in the pair is the opposite color from the first stitch in the previous pair.

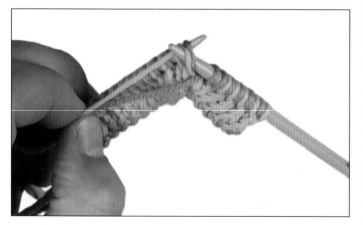

2) ... and likewise, the purl stitch is the opposite color from the second stitch in the previous pair, completing the color change.

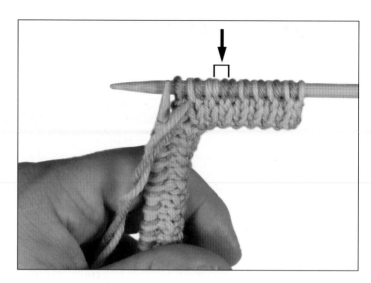

3) Here is the color change completed, a few pairs back. Note that the pair is reversed in color configuration from the other pairs in the row. This creates the illusion of two same-colored pairs next to each other, but in fact those four stitches are two in a pair, surrounded by two stitches from the previous and next pairs.

Because you will not see the effect of a row with color-changing in it until the following row is worked (the loops still being on the needle), you may find it difficult to read your knitting to double-check that your row was worked correctly. See the section on reading your double-knitting on page 167.

As you begin to change colors, you may notice that your active ends will begin to twist around each other. The more you change colors, the twistier the ends will get. This is because most double-knitters have a tendency to rotate their ends in one direction or another. Every time you make a color change, your ends change places — the color that was facing goes to the opposite side, and vice versa. While you might not notice it, this implies a 180-degree twist with every color change. These add up and cause the ends to twist around each other. However, it doesn't matter which way you twist the ends — clockwise or counterclockwise, front over back or back over front. If you can keep the presence of mind to twist in one direction when changing from Color A to Color B on the facing side, and twist in the other direction when changing from Color B to Color A, you will diminish the effect of the twist. The twists created at the edges of flat work will still occur, and you can compensate for those either by twisting an extra color change in the opposite direction, or periodically releasing your source yarn balls and untwisting the other end.

ADDING A NEW SKEIN

At some point you will probably wind up at the end of your yarn (which is a bit different from being at the end of your rope, usually) and will need to add a new skein. Because skeins are not usually perfectly measured, and because your gauge may not be perfectly the same on either side, you probably won't run out of any two colors at the same time.

There are a number of ways to add a new skein, but this is the one I prefer.

1) Work until you have a reasonable amount of yarn to weave in afterward, and, if you're working flat, you're somewhere in the middle of a row. If this means you have a little more of an end than you'd prefer, that's better than having too little.

2) Let the end stick out of the side opposite its own side — if the end is Color A and your current stitch is Color A on the facing side, let the end stick out of the opposite side.

3) Take the new end and lay it alongside the old end, then work the rest of the row or round with the new end.

4) Work a couple more rows, being careful of the loose loops associated with the short ends when you get to them.

5) Turn the knitting so you can see the ends. Tie a loose overhand knot. Tighten only enough so that the knot goes down to the base of the two ends. Keep an eye on the stitches the ends come out of to make sure they don't get distorted. Weave in both ends (see the chapter on finishing, page 158)

READING STANDARD DOUBLE-KNITTING CHARTS IN THE FLAT AND IN THE ROUND

Since every pattern in this book involves a color chart of some kind, it will behoove you to learn to read double-knit charts properly. Most double-knit charts are the same as any other stranded knitting chart, but only the facing side is shown. The opposite side — reversed in color and orientation — is implied. While working in the round, you will see the chart you are reading form in your knitting — and as long as the corresponding purl stitch of every pair is done in the opposite color from the knit stitch, you will end up with the same chart on the opposite side, reversed.

In flat double-knitting, however, when you turn your work and facing and opposite switch sides, you will need to mentally reverse the color and orientation of the chart — in other words, follow the opposite-side rows from left to right and in the opposite colors from the way the chart is written. For more on reading double-knitting charts, see the section on Reading your Double-Knitting, page 167.

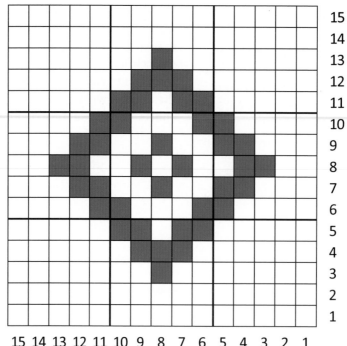

15
14
13
12
11
10
9
8
7
6
5
4
3
2
1

15 14 13 12 11 10 9 8 7 6 5 4 3 2 1

EXERCISE: DIAMOND

This is the pattern I teach in my Double-knitting Level 1 workshops. It's a great starter pattern for a number of reasons — it's small, so it won't take very long; it's symmetrical, so you don't have to think as much about the opposite-side rows; and it makes a great gauge swatch if you have another project in mind with the same yarn and needles.

Using two colors of plain worsted or DK-weight yarn and appropriately-sized needles, cast on 15 pairs or 30 total stitches using the standard double-knit cast-on. Your darker color will be the FC and your lighter color will be the TC. Work the pattern as charted, remembering to twist your edge stitches and keeping in mind the reversal of colors on the opposite-side rows. You can work the selvedge for the last pair in each row if you like.

After the last row, work the standard double-knit bind-off in colors matching the row below.

If following charts is not your strong suit, see the chapter on Reading your Double-Knitting for a verbal translation of this chart. However, the rest of the patterns in this book are chart-only, so it would be best if you learned to do that translation mentally yourself.

EXERCISE: DIAMOND IN THE ROUND

Because there are more patterns in this book that deal with double-knitting in the round than flat, you may also want to try this pattern in the round. For this, you'll want to follow the pattern at least twice.

Using two colors of plain worsted or DK-weight yarn and an appropriately-sized circular needle or DPNs, cast on a multiple of 15 pairs using the standard double-knit cast-on. Your lighter color will be your FC, and your darker color will be your TC. If you're using DPNs, divide your pairs evenly. Join the ends, being careful not to twist the cast-on edge and follow the pattern as charted. Note that while following this pattern in the round, you do not have to reverse colors and directions every other round — the facing side is always the side shown in the pattern.

After the last round, work the standard double-knit bind-off in colors matching the round below.

Alternatively, you can stop part way through the pattern and hold this sample to the side for use in the exercise on double-knitting with two circular needles (see page 136).

PATTERN: CORVUS

(aka the Crow Scarf) Sample knit by Beth Levine

This was the very first double-knitting project I designed and started. The pattern has gone through some revisions, and the previous revision is actually available for free as a Ravelry download. I originally designed it for my sister Margaret, who was at the time obsessed with crows, ravens and other unusually intelligent black birds. I charted the crow design itself from a photo I found online of a crow perched on a wire. I have knit two of these, one as a gift and one for a commission, and after the last I vowed never to knit another. I added the marching crow's feet up and down the sides of the scarf to relieve the boredom of working 4+ feet of plain double-stockinette, but I still find the process tedious. However, it is a very elegant and unisex scarf, perfect for the bird-lover or goth in your life.

MATERIALS:

[Color A] Berroco Ultra Alpaca (50% Super Fine Alpaca/50% Peruvian Wool); 215 yds/100g skein; #6214: Steel Cut Oats; 2 skeins. 9 wpi.
[Color B] Berroco Ultra Alpaca (50% Super Fine Alpaca/50% Peruvian Wool); 215 yds/100g skein; #6245: Pitch Black; 2 skeins. 9 wpi

1 set US6/4mm straight needles, or needle size required to achieve gauge.
Tapestry needle

GAUGE:

20 sts/28 rows = 4" in double-stockinette fabric. Since this garment is not sized, gauge is not critical.

PATTERN NOTES AND IDEAS:

The crow chart is also a really nice large motif for intarsia or duplicate stitch work on a sweater.

If you want to try double-knit corrugated ribbing for the mock rib section at the ends of this scarf, check the Appendix (page 183) for instructions.

PATTERN:

Cast on 32 pairs or 64 total stitches, using the standard cast-on method, with Color A as FC and Color B as TC. Turn.

Follow Chart 1 for 16 rows (or however many or few you prefer). At the end of the first row, remember to remove and untie the slip knot.

Follow Chart 2 for 4 rows. Keep in mind that your facing-side selvedge will change color configuration here.

Work Chart 3.

Follow Chart 2 for 6 rows.

Repeat Chart 4 until you don't have enough yarn to finish another repeat. You can stop early if you want a shorter scarf or you're tired of working on it — but you might as well finish because you're only halfway there.

Count your Chart 4 repeats. Work the same number of repeats again, switching to the second pair of skeins when necessary. This is done to make the scarf as long as possible while guaranteeing you won't run out of yarn!

Follow Chart 2 for 4 rows.

Work Chart 5.

Follow Chart 2 for 4 rows.
Follow Chart 1 for the same number of rows as you started with. Bind off and weave in all ends.

CHART 1

| 32 | 31 | 30 | 29 | 28 | 27 | 26 | 25 | 24 | 23 | 22 | 21 | 20 | 19 | 18 | 17 | 16 | 15 | 14 | 13 | 12 | 11 | 10 | 9 | 8 | 7 | 6 | 5 | 4 | 3 | 2 | 1 |

CHART 2

| 32 | 31 | 30 | 29 | 28 | 27 | 26 | 25 | 24 | 23 | 22 | 21 | 20 | 19 | 18 | 17 | 16 | 15 | 14 | 13 | 12 | 11 | 10 | 9 | 8 | 7 | 6 | 5 | 4 | 3 | 2 | 1 |

CHART 3

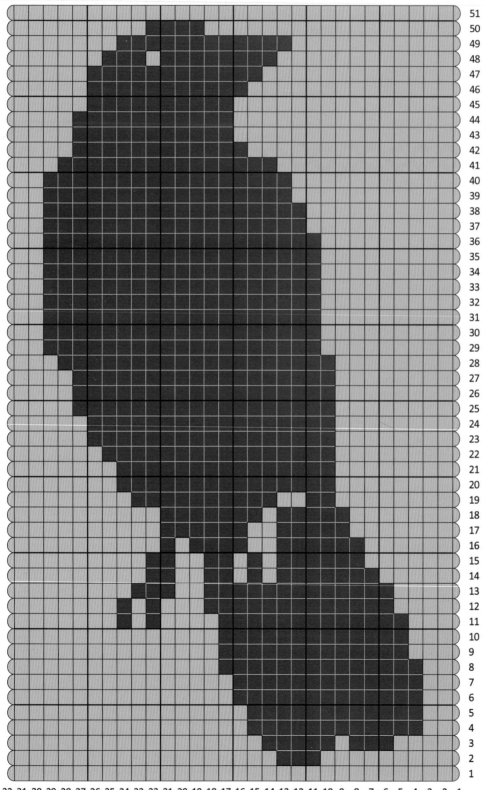

32 31 30 29 28 27 26 25 24 23 22 21 20 19 18 17 16 15 14 13 12 11 10 9 8 7 6 5 4 3 2 1

CHART KEY

Color A	
Color B	
◖	Color B selvedge at end of facing-side row
◖	Color A selvedge at end of facing-side row
◗	Color B selvedge at end of opposite-side row

CHART 4

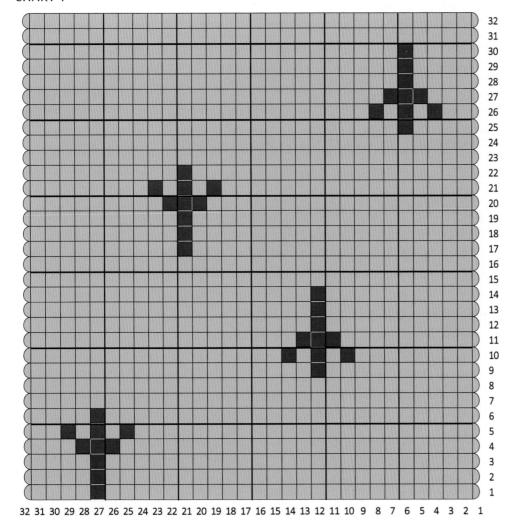

CHART 5

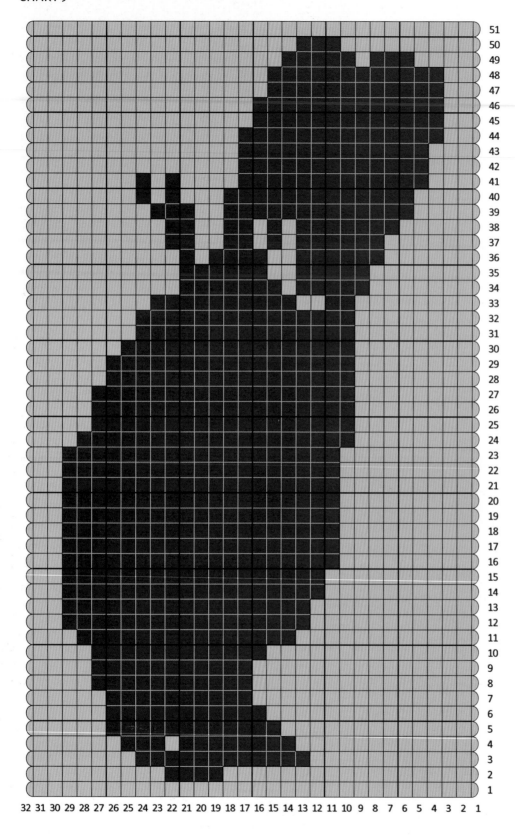

PATTERN: SIERPINSKI

Sample knitted by Stacey Trock

The Sierpinski Carpet is a type of fractal — meaning, in simple terms, that it is a shape made up of smaller copies of itself, which are in turn made up of smaller copies, and so on ad infinitum. Fractals can be simplified by only extending them to a certain iteration — and some simplified fractals can be charted for knitting. This fractal is created by starting with a square, then dividing it in 9ths (with a 3x3 grid) and removing the center square. Further iterations are created by subdividing the resulting squares, etc.

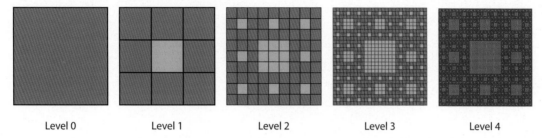

| Level 0 | Level 1 | Level 2 | Level 3 | Level 4 |

My original idea was to build a Level-5 Sierpinski carpet, but at 251 pairs square, it would have created a 45-inch square throw blanket, whereas I was targeting a baby blanket. So I redesigned it so it would have a Level 4 fractal surrounded by Level 3s, surrounded by Level 2s. At about 33 inches square after blocking, this came out just about right.

MATERIALS:

[Color A] Cascade 220 Superwash (100% Peruvian Highland Wool; Superwash Treated); 220 yds/100g skein; #877; 4 skeins. 9 wpi.
[Color B] Cascade 220 Superwash (100% Peruvian Highland Wool; Superwash Treated); 220 yds/100g skein; #1947; 4 skeins. 9 wpi.

1 36-inch US6/4mm circular needle, or needle size required to attain gauge desired.
Tapestry needle

GAUGE:

22 sts/30 rows = 4" in double-stockinette fabric (unblocked). Since this item is not sized, gauge is not critical.

PATTERN NOTES AND IDEAS:

If you are a glutton for punishment and/or a big math geek, try a Level 5 Sierpinski Carpet pattern by taking the Level 4 at the center of this blanket and tiling it in the same way. This should give you 243 cast-on pairs, assuming no border. My original idea was to use Cascade Eco rather than 220, which, at a gauge of 3.5-4 sts/in, would give you a 60-70" square blanket, at least the width of a queen-size bed. For comparison, a Level 6 in the same yarn would cover the floor of a 225 square foot living room — at which point it really would become a Sierpinski Carpet.

PATTERN:

Cast on 181 pairs or 362 total stitches using the standard double-knit cast-on, with Color B as FC and Color A as TC. Before starting, remove the slip knot from the beginning of your cast-on row. Working flat, with selvedge pairs as charted, follow the 9 charts in sequence: 1a, 1b, 1c; 2a, 2b, 2c; 3a, 3b, 3c. Bind off with standard double-knit bind-off. Block to square, weave in ends and enjoy!

	Color A
	Color B
	Selvedge at end of facing-side row
	Selvedge at end of opposite-side row

CHART 1a

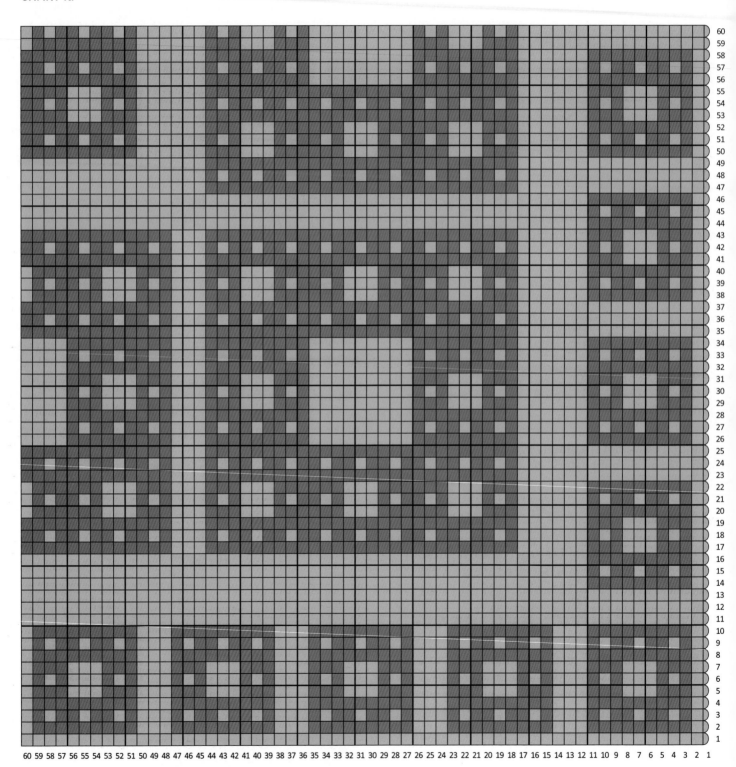

60 59 58 57 56 55 54 53 52 51 50 49 48 47 46 45 44 43 42 41 40 39 38 37 36 35 34 33 32 31 30 29 28 27 26 25 24 23 22 21 20 19 18 17 16 15 14 13 12 11 10 9 8 7 6 5 4 3 2 1

CHART 1b

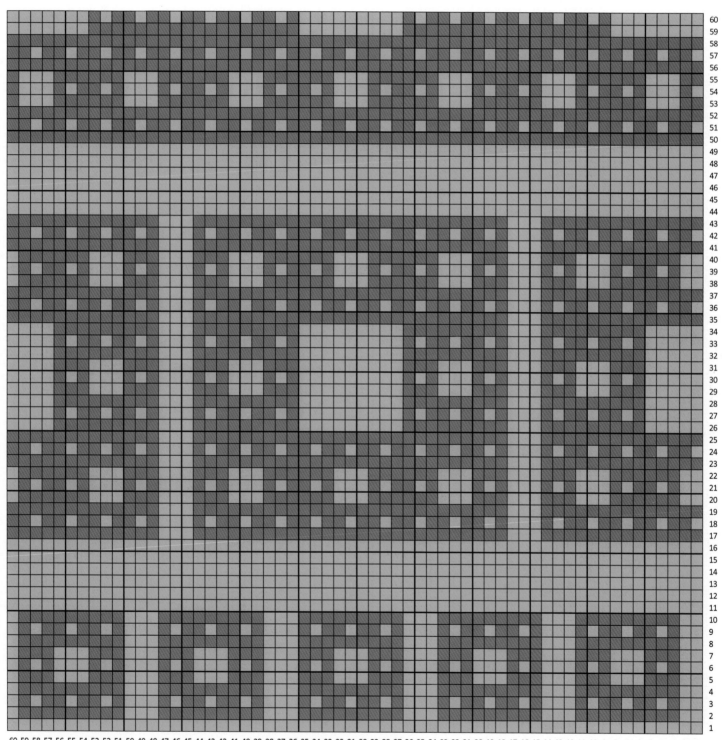

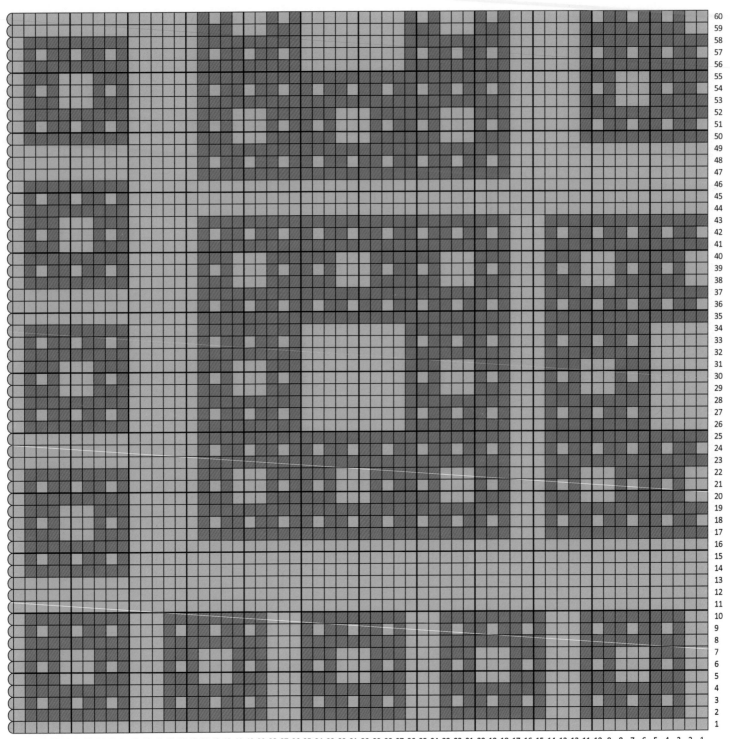

CHART 2a

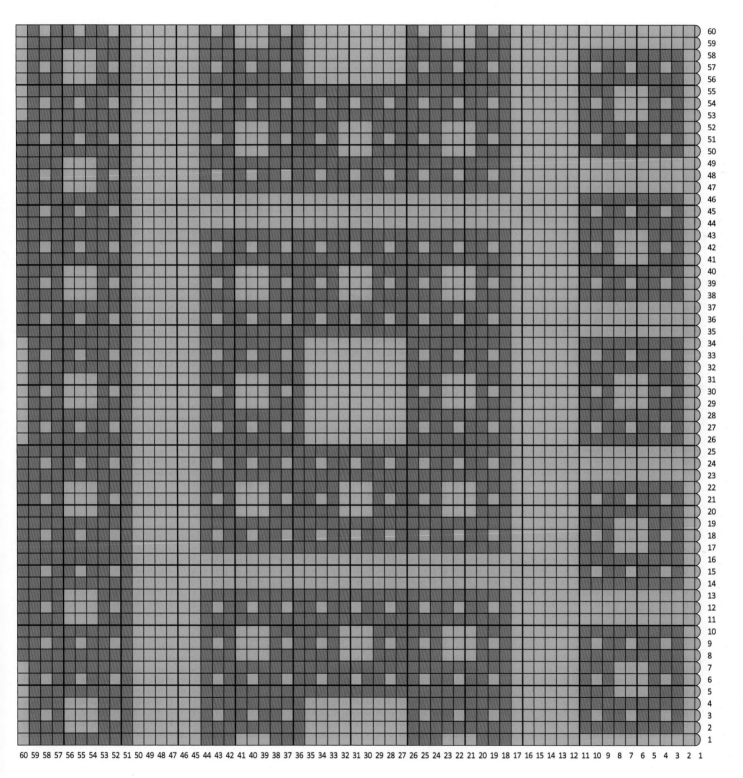

CHART 2b

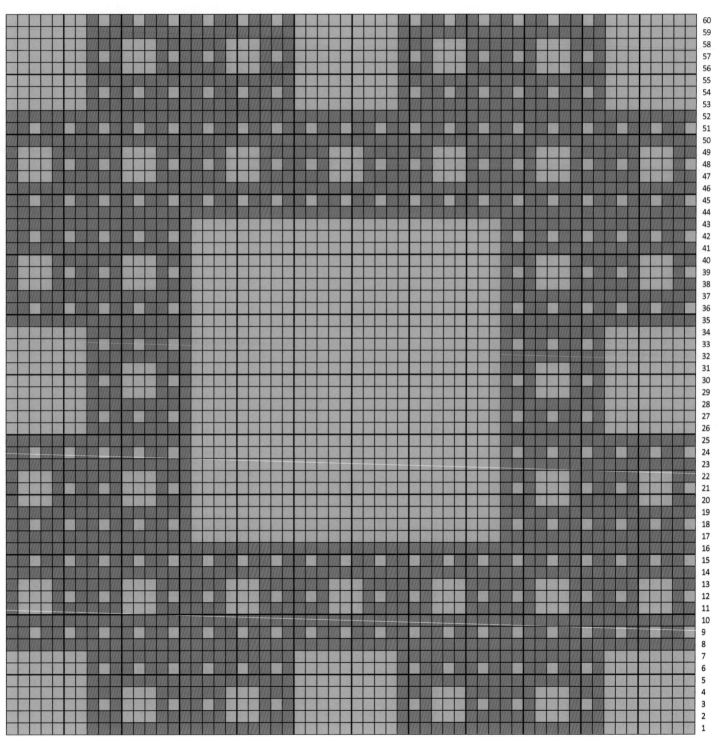

CHART 2c

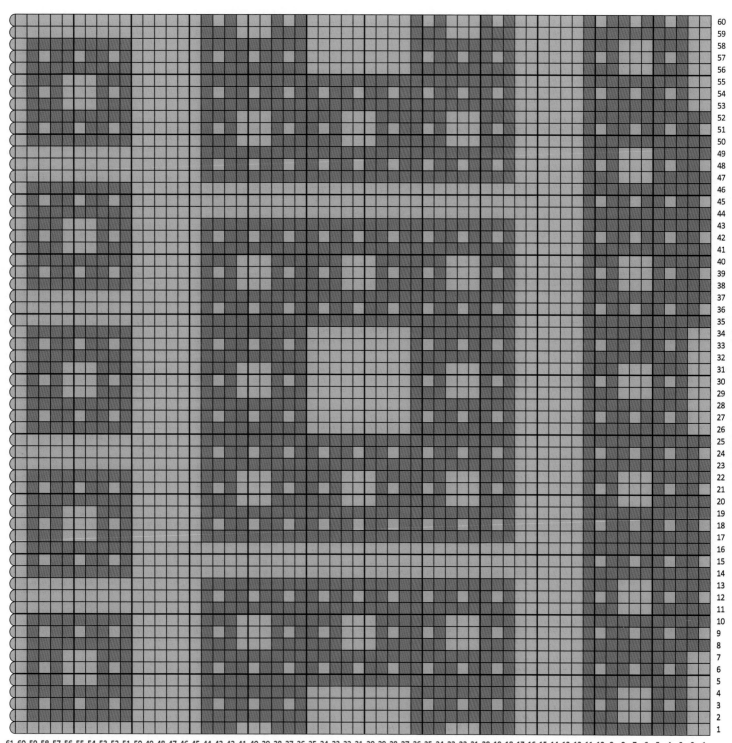

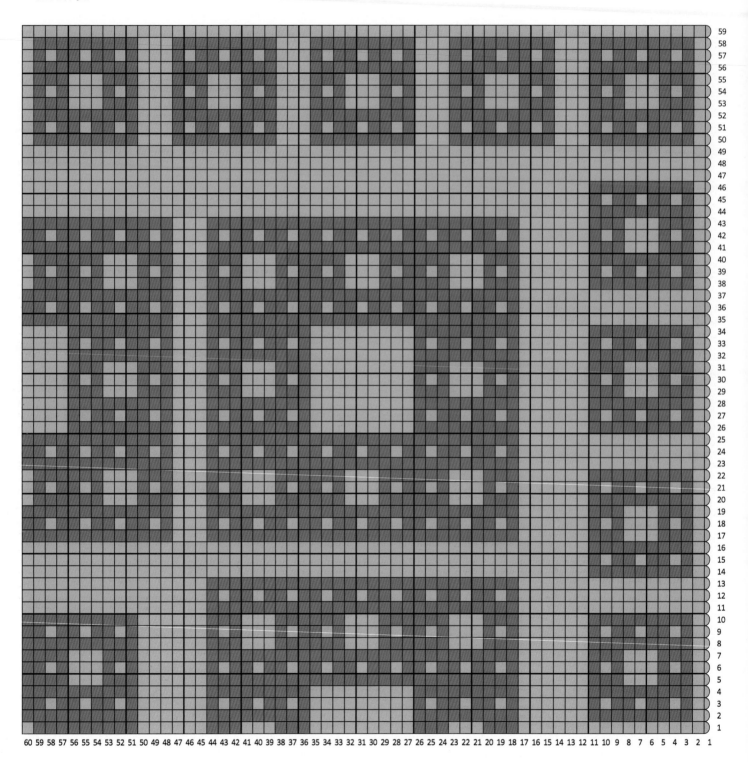

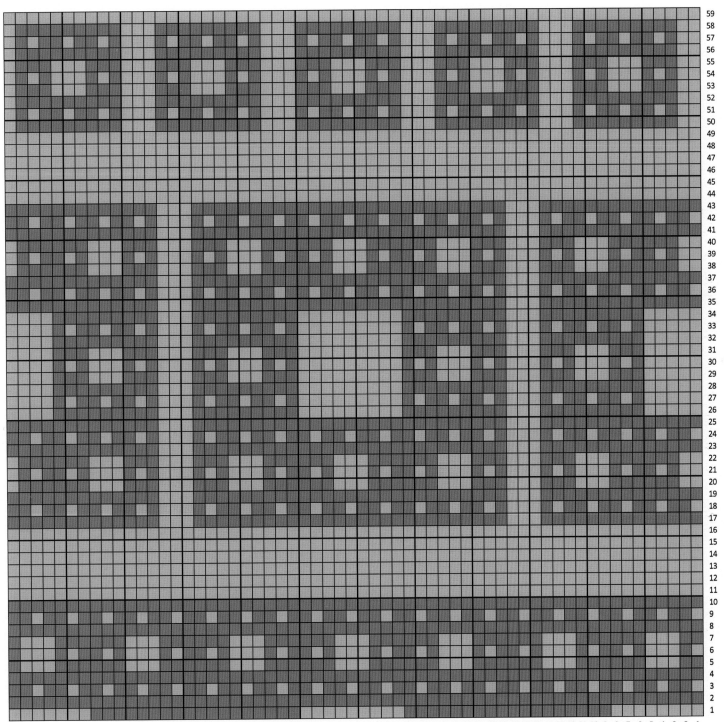

CHART 3c

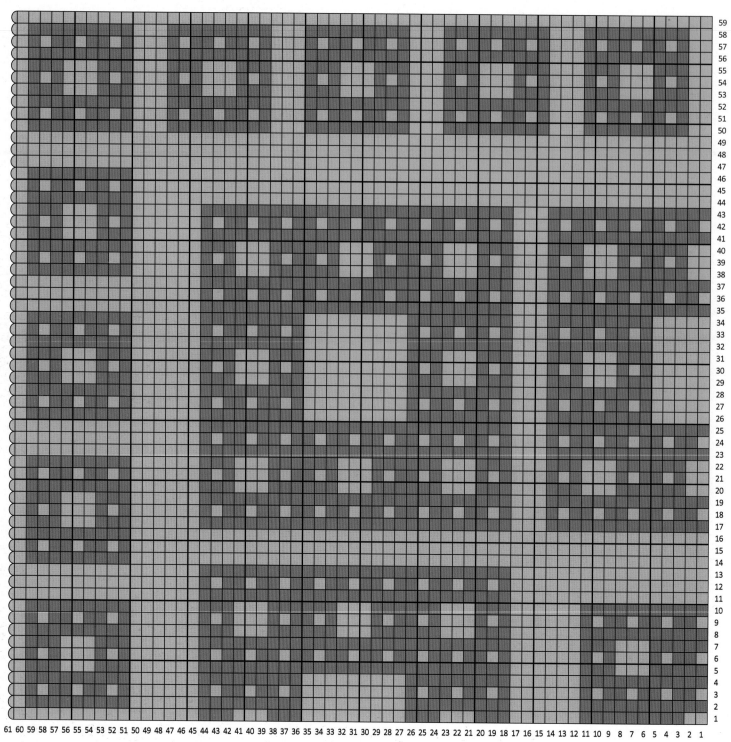

PATTERN: WRIST CHAKRA

Sample knit by Alasdair Post-Quinn

These quick and simple wristwarmers are a great warm-up for double-knitting in the round, without the commitment of yarn and time and technique learning that a hat represents. They're based on a spiral found in an inexpensive but quite comprehensive Celtic chart book by Co Spinhoven.

MATERIALS:

[Color A] Araucania Nature Wool (100% Wool); 242 yds/100g skein; #62; 1 skein. 9 wpi.
[Color B] Araucania Nature Wool (100% Wool); 242 yds/100g skein; #50; 1 skein. 9 wpi.

1 set US5/4mm DPNs, or needle size required to achieve gauge desired.
Tapestry needle

GAUGE:

24 sts/32 rows = 4" in double-stockinette fabric.

PATTERN NOTES AND IDEAS:

There are 7 chakra points in the Hindu religion, and used by energy workers and those who practice certain types of meditation. However, those 7 are only the "pools" where the chakra builds up. There are many more minor chakra points acknowledged. If you like, you can expand the number of cast-on pairs and make a headband out of this pattern — the "Third Eye Chakra".

PATTERN:

Measure the wrists you intend to make these for. A 7" circumference is about average. If your wrists are larger, add more pairs as needed according to your gauge. They will be added to the background at the end of the pattern. If your wrists are smaller, try using size 4 or smaller needles to achieve a smaller gauge (more sts/in), then recalculating and adding more pairs if needed. This will also change your row gauge, so feel free to add rounds of plain background double-stockinette at the bottom and top of the chart if you like.

For wrists measuring 7 (8, 9) inches, cast on 43 (49, 55) pairs or 86 (98, 110) total stitches in standard double-knitting cast-on with Color A as FC and Color B as TC. Divide onto 3 or 4 DPNs; join ends of the work, being careful not to twist the cast-on edge.

Follow Chart 1 in double-knitting, adding any extra columns to the end of the chart in the background color configuration (Color A facing, Color B opposite).

Bind off using standard double-knit bind-off and weave in ends.

Repeat a second time. Optionally, reverse all colors in the instructions above and follow Chart 2 (and then turn inside out) for a mirror image in the same colors on your other wrist. If you like, you can follow Chart 1 again, and if you want a mirror image you can turn the wristwarmer inside out.

 Color A

 Color B

CHART 1

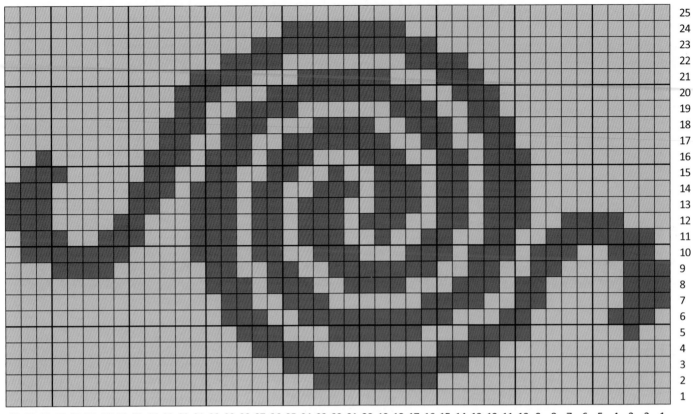

25 24 23 22 21 20 19 18 17 16 15 14 13 12 11 10 9 8 7 6 5 4 3 2 1

43 42 41 40 39 38 37 36 35 34 33 32 31 30 29 28 27 26 25 24 23 22 21 20 19 18 17 16 15 14 13 12 11 10 9 8 7 6 5 4 3 2 1

CHART 2

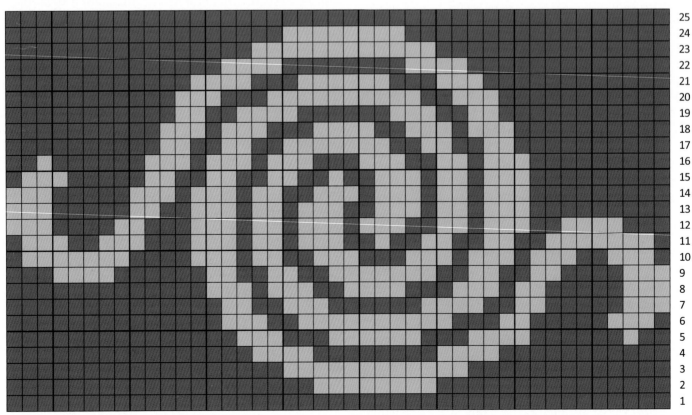

25 24 23 22 21 20 19 18 17 16 15 14 13 12 11 10 9 8 7 6 5 4 3 2 1

43 42 41 40 39 38 37 36 35 34 33 32 31 30 29 28 27 26 25 24 23 22 21 20 19 18 17 16 15 14 13 12 11 10 9 8 7 6 5 4 3 2 1

CHAPTER 3: DOUBLE-KNIT SHAPING

It would hardly be true to say that any plain knit or colorworked garment can be translated to double-knitting without taking into account the shaping that must be done. Adding increases and decreases to your repertoire is vital for shaping — but it's also fun to add them in for decorative purposes. Adding a decrease and an increase in rapid succession can appear to move a pair sideways. As long as the number of pairs subtracted equals the number added, the row or round will stay the same size.

DECREASING

Decreasing in double-knitting requires a little bit of stitch reordering. Currently, your stitches run knit-purl repeated ad infinitum. In order to decrease, you need to temporarily separate the layers and put two or three knit stitches together, next to two or three purl stitches. You will then decrease (or double-decrease) those groups of stitches to make a single pair again.

Single decreases — 2 pairs into 1 — are generally considered to be either left-slanting or right-slanting. As a matter of fact, these are misnomers — the difference between the decreases is not which way they slant, but which of the two stitches ends up on top. It's how they're positioned relative to other decreases and pattern elements that dictates how they slant. I frequently use "left-slanting" decreases to send a group of pairs to the right or vice versa, depending on how I want the design to look.

SINGLE DECREASE SETUP

Both types of single decreases are set up in the same way, in order to reorder 2 pairs from K-P-K-P to K-K-P-P:

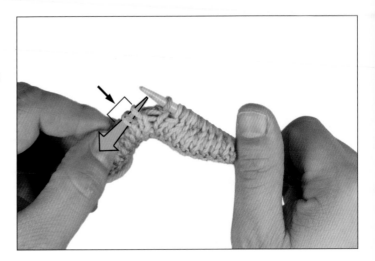

1) The two pairs in the bracket are the two which will be prepared for a decrease. First, insert your right needle purlwise into the first three stitches on the left needle.

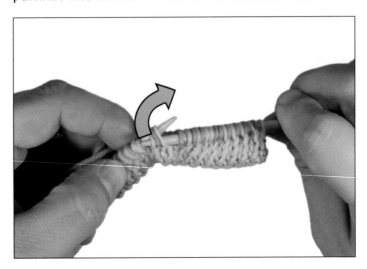

2) Slip those three stitches onto the right needle. Leave the last stitch in the second pair on the left needle. You can do this all at once or one by one, as long as you keep them all slipped purlwise.

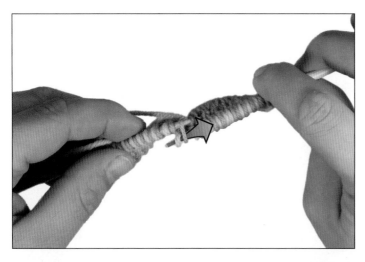

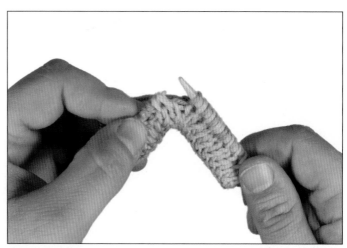

3) Insert the left needle into the second stitch on the right needle from the back. Pull the right needle out of two stitches, leaving the first slipped stitch on the needle. Make sure to hold the base of the loose stitch with your thumb.

The same two pairs are shown here, now reordered for decreasing.

You can assist steps 3 and 4 with a cable needle to hold the loose stitch, but in general it's not needed for only a single stitch.

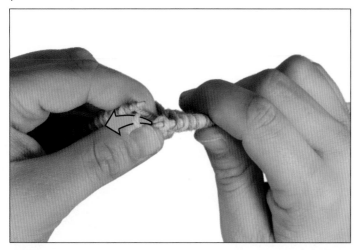

4) Insert the right needle into the loose knit stitch.

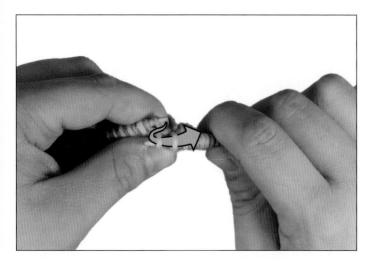

5) Pass two stitches from the right needle to the left.

LEFT-SLANTING DECREASE (RIGHT STITCH ON TOP)

Untwisted

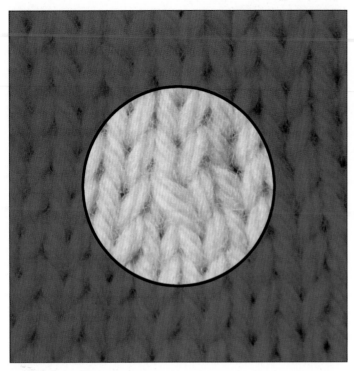

Twisted

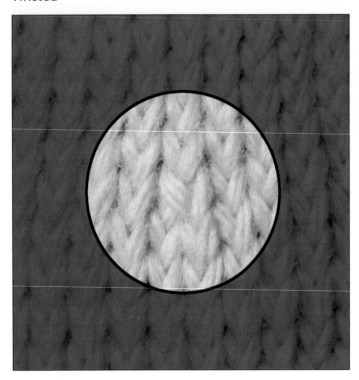

The simple way to think of this decrease is like this:

1)   Wyib, SSK
2)   Wyif, P2Tog

But if you are not familiar with single-faced decrease methods, you can follow the step-by-step instructions until you're more comfortable:

SSK:

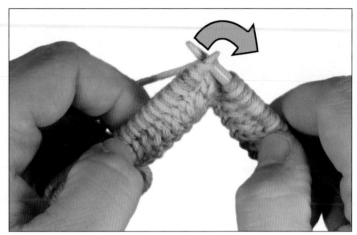

1) With both ends in back, slip the first stitch knitwise.

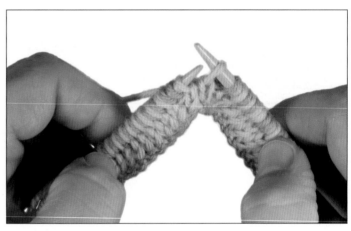

2) Slip the second stitch knitwise as well.

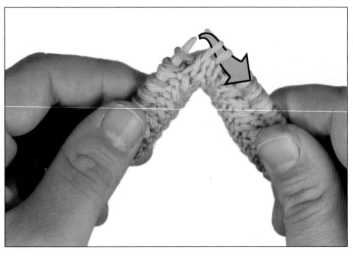

3) Insert the left needle into the two loops on the right needle, keeping the left needle in front, but leave the right needle in the loops.

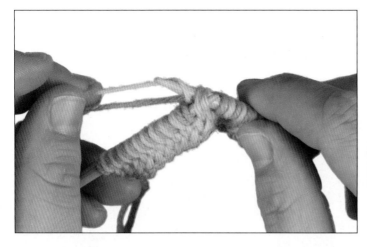

4) Knit the color indicated by the pattern to complete the SSK.

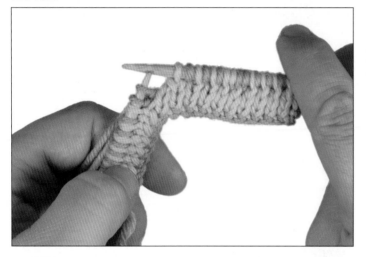

5) Note that the right stitch is on top, which slants the decrease to the left on the facing side. (next page)

P2TOG:

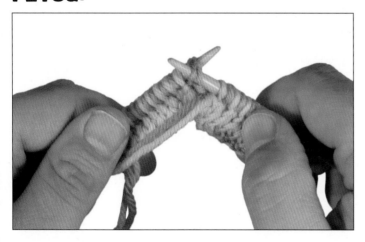

6) Bring both ends to the front and insert the right needle purlwise through both purl loops on the left needle.

7) Purl with the color indicated by the pattern to complete the P2Tog.

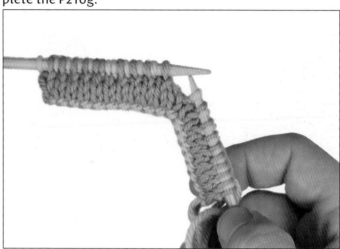

8) Note that the decrease on the opposite side slants to the right — the mirror image of the decrease on the facing side.

RIGHT-SLANTING DECREASE (LEFT STITCH ON TOP)

Far fewer people are familiar with the SSP technique than the more common SSK above. If you don't know it, feel free to follow the step-by step instructions below.

Untwisted

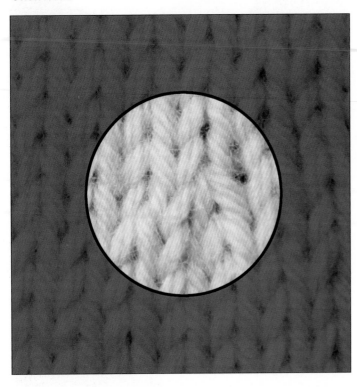

K2TOG:

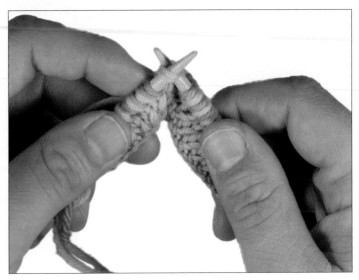

1) With both ends in back, insert your right needle through both knit stitches and knit them together with the color indicated by the pattern.

Twisted

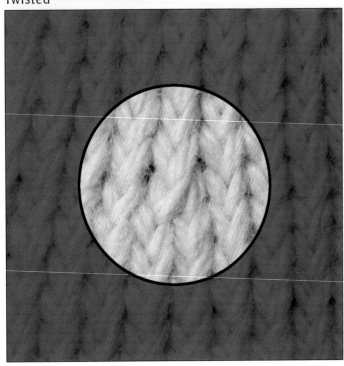

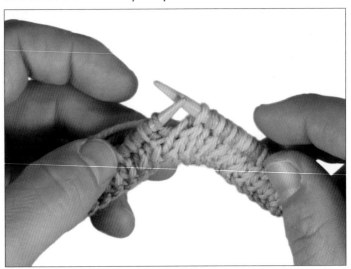

2) You can see that the left stitch in the pair is on top, and the decrease slants to the right on the facing side of the work.

The simple way to think of this decrease is like this:

1)   Wyib, K2Tog
2)   Wyif, SSP

SSP:

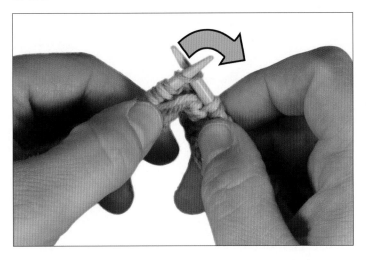

3) Bring both ends to the front. Slip the next stitch as if to knit. Do this for the second stitch as well — you are slipping them separately, not together.

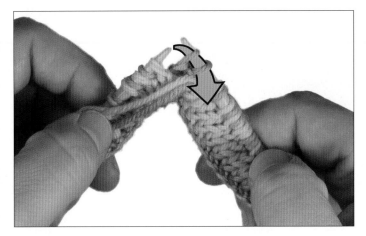

4) Pass two stitches back to the left needle.

5) Insert the right needle through both stitches from the back.

6) Purl with the color indicated by the pattern. This is a P2TogTBL (purl 2 together through the back loops).

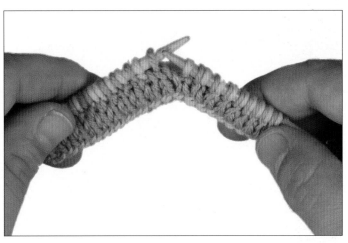

7) You can see that the decrease on the opposite side slants to the left — the mirror image of the decrease on the facing side.

It is important to remember that the direction of the purl decrease will be a mirror image of the knit decrease. You want them to slant in the same direction. Other instructions may tell you to simply K2Tog, then P2Tog to complete the pair, but this decreases in two directions and frankly lacks attention to detail that is easily achieved by adding two more types of decrease in the proper places.

There is another way to do these decreases which integrates the pair reordering and does not require any stitches to be dropped and picked up. However, because I have not found a reasonable way to do the double-decrease setup with the same methods, these other methods are outlined in the Appendix (page 180).

DOUBLE DECREASES

Double decreases — 3 pairs into 1 — are characterized by their symmetry. Technically, k3tog and SSSP are double decreases, but I find those inelegant. So far I have had more use for double decreases that slant inward to a center point. The distinction between the two double decreases used in this book is the positioning of the center stitch — either on top or on bottom.

DOUBLE DECREASE SETUP

Both types of double decreases are set up the same way, in order to reorder 3 pairs from K-P-K-P-K-P to K-K-K-P-P-P.

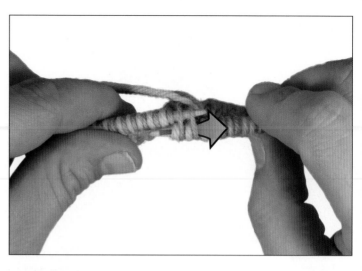

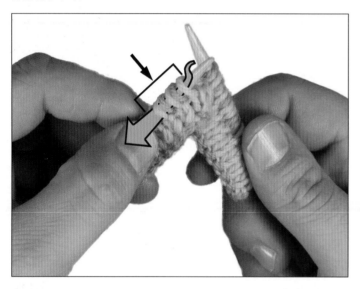

1) The three pairs in the bracket are the three which will be prepared for a double-decrease. First, insert your right needle purlwise into the first five stitches on the left needle.

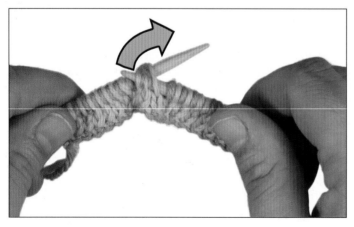

2) Slip those five stitches onto the right needle. Leave the last stitch in the third pair on the left needle. You can do this all at once or one by one, as long as you keep them all slipped purlwise.

3) Insert left needle into the 2nd and 4th stitches on the right needle from the back. Pull the right needle out of four stitches, leaving the first slipped stitch on the needle. Make sure to hold the base of the two loose stitches with your thumb.

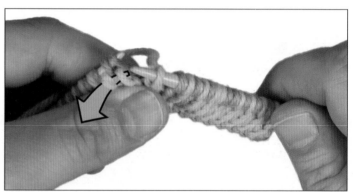

4) Insert the right needle into the loose knit stitches.

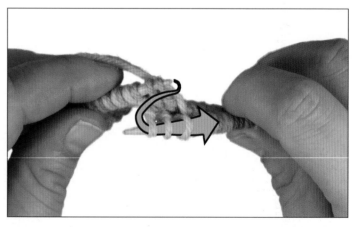

5) Pass 3 stitches from the right needle to the left needle.

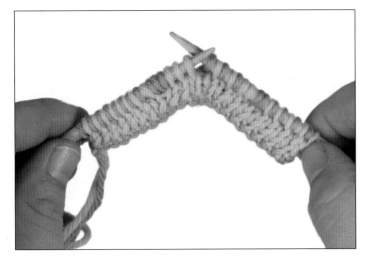

The same three pairs are shown here, now reordered for double-decreasing.

Steps 3 and 4 can be assisted with a cable needle to hold the two loose stitches, if you like, but I've generally found that non-slippery yarns like wool are up to the task of not losing stitches easily.

STANDARD DOUBLE DECREASE (CENTER STITCH ON BOTTOM)

Untwisted

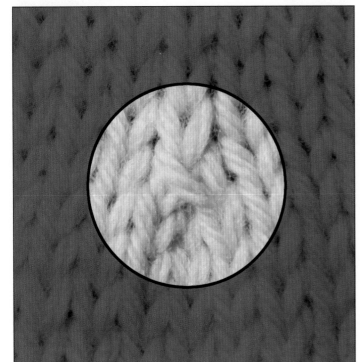

Twisted

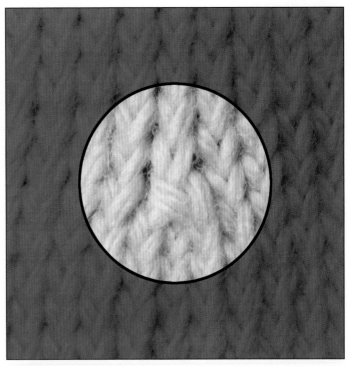

Facing side:

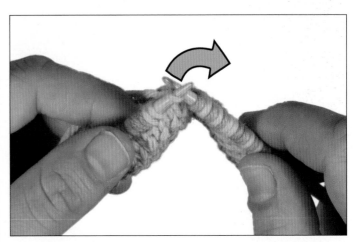

1) With both ends in back, slip 1 stitch knitwise.

2) Knit the next 2 stitches together (K2Tog) with the color indicated by the pattern.

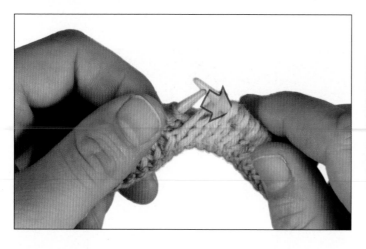

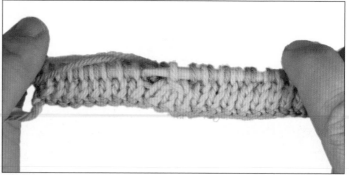

3) Insert your left needle into the second stitch on the right needle …

6) This is the double-decrease on the facing side. You can see that the decrease is centered, and that the center stitch is on the bottom, with the left and right stitches layered on top of it.

Opposite side:

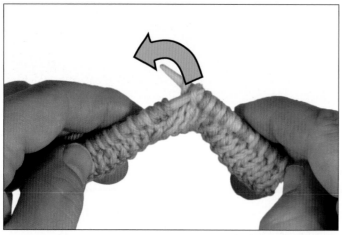

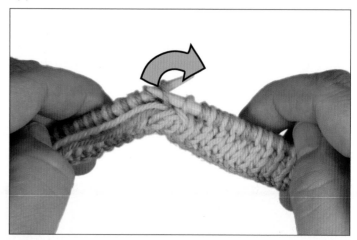

4) …and pull it over the first stitch and off the needle (PSSO)

7) Bring both ends to the front. Slip the first stitch purlwise.

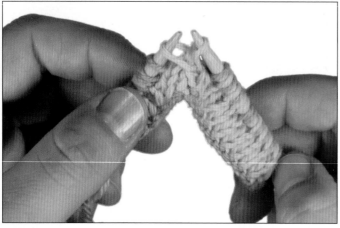

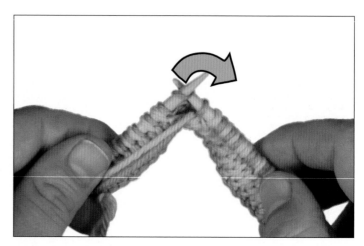

5) This is the same procedure, in progress.

8) Slip the second and third stitches separately knitwise (only the first is illustrated)

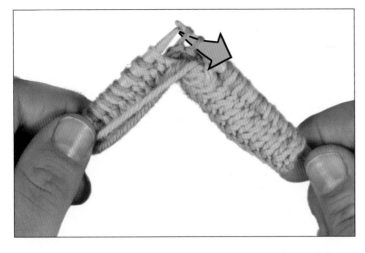

9) Pass the last two slipped stitches back to the left needle.

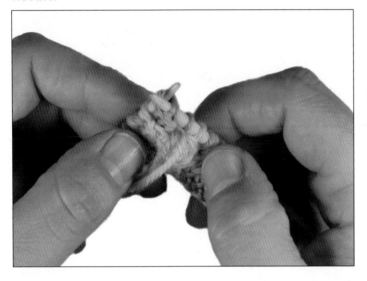

10) Insert the right needle into both stitches on the left needle from the back. (Next page)

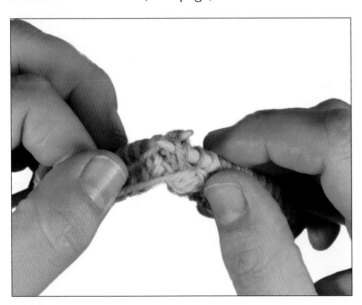

11) Purl 2 together (P2TogTBL) with the color indicated in the pattern.

12) Insert the left needle into the second stitch on the right needle …

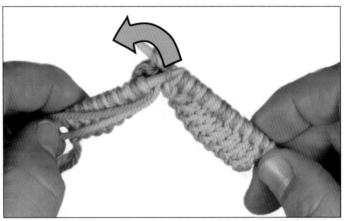

13) …and pull it over the first stitch and off the needle (PSSO).

14) This is the same procedure, in progress.

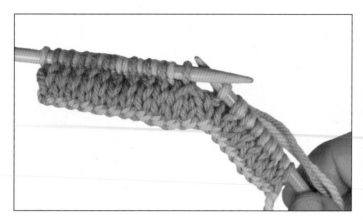

15) You can see on the opposite side that this decrease is the mirror image of the one on the facing side. Although they are symmetrical in structure, one of the side stitches has to be on top of the other — on the facing side, it's the right stitch; on the opposite side it's the left one.

RIDGED DOUBLE DECREASE (CENTER STITCH ON TOP)

Untwisted

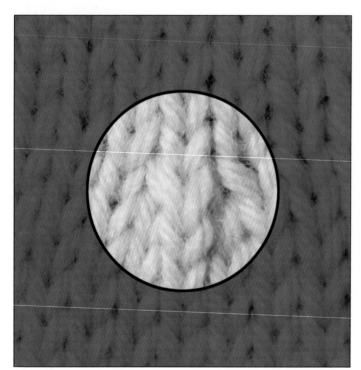

Twisted

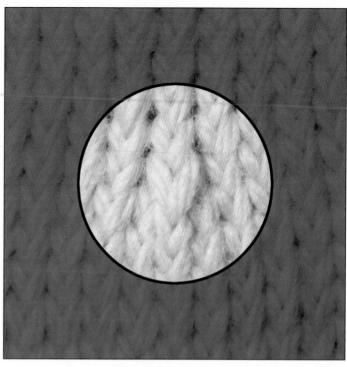

Facing side:

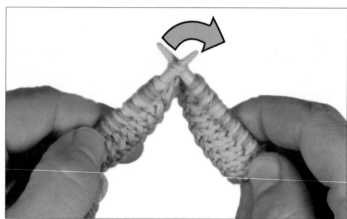

1) With both ends in back, insert your right needle into the first two stitches knitwise, then slip them together onto the right needle

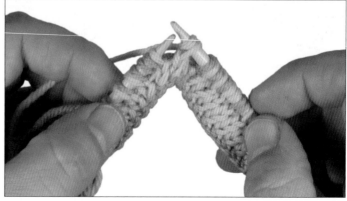

2) ... like so. (Sl2Tog)

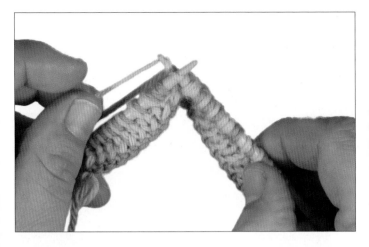

3) Knit the next stitch with the color indicated by the pattern.

4) Insert your left needle into the second and third stitches on the right needle. They should be twisted together from the Sl2Tog in step 1.

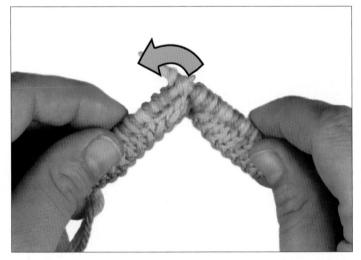

5) Pull both stitches over the first stitch and off the needle (P2SO).

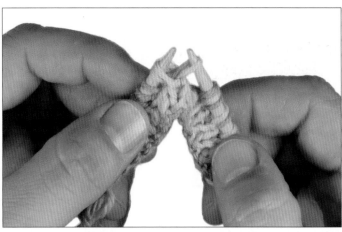

6) This is the same procedure, in progress.

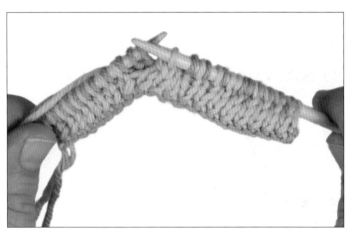

7) The finished double-decrease on the facing side. You can see that the center stitch is on top and the other two are layered underneath it.

Opposite side:

8) Bring both ends to the front. Slip the next two stitches separately knitwise (only the first is illustrated here).

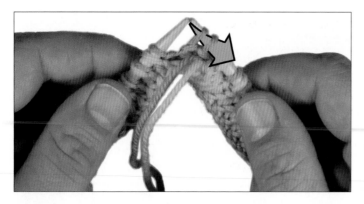

9) Pass both slipped stitches back to the left needle.

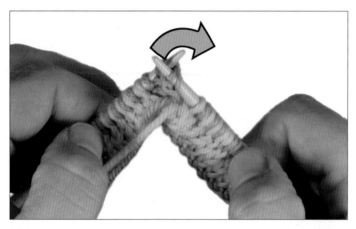

10) Insert the right needle into both stitches from the back, and slip them off and onto the right needle. (Sl2TogTBL)

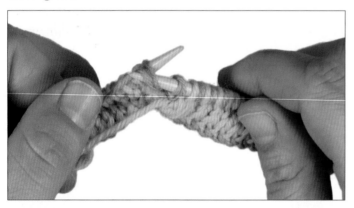

11) Purl the next stitch with the color indicated by the pattern.

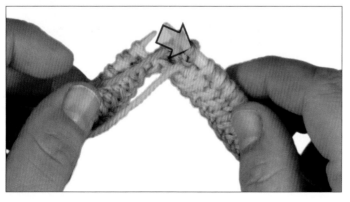

12) Insert your left needle into the second and third stitches on the right needle. They should be twisted together from the Sl2TogTBL.

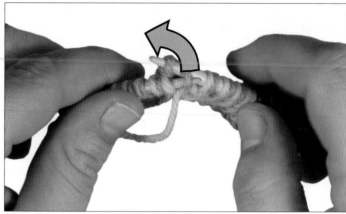

13) Pull both stitches over the first stitch and off the needle (P2SO).

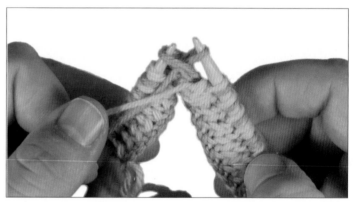

14) This is the same procedure, in progress.

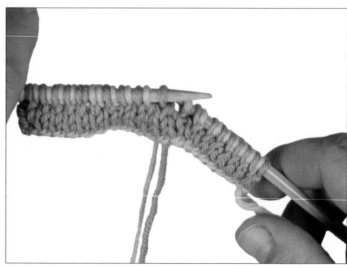

15) This is the completed double-decrease on the opposite side.

Pay careful attention to your tension after doing either of these; the ridged double decrease in particular is prone to tension differences between the two sides.

FOLLOWING DECREASES IN DOUBLE-KNITTING CHARTS

In many of the charts in this book, decreases are used as decorative elements rather than simply for shaping. It is important to pay attention to the placement and color-ation of the decrease chart elements. For single de-creases, the placement refers to the stitch which will be on top — for a right-slanting decrease, the chart element will be placed above the leftmost of the two pixels below it; for a left-slanting decrease, the chart element will be placed above the rightmost of the two pixels below it. The color of the pixel the chart element is on represents the color that should be used for the knit stitch of the pair when the decrease is made; the purl stitch will be the opposite color unless otherwise indicated.

 Left-slanting decrease

 Right-slanting decrease

 Double decrease

For double decreases, the placement refers to the stitch which will be at the center, and the symbol indicates whether the center stitch will be on top or bottom. The three pixels — one directly below the center stitch and one in the row below and to each side are the pairs that will be reordered, and the color of the pixel the chart el-ement is on represents the color that should be used for the knit stitch of the pair when the decrease is made; the purl stitch will be the opposite color unless otherwise indicated.

INCREASING

Without increases, your double-knitting rows or rounds will just get smaller and smaller — which is all well and good for a hat, but for other types of shaping you'll want to make more pairs rather than fewer. Increasing in dou-ble-knitting is much easier than decreasing, since there is no reordering of pairs. You simply make an increase on the facing side and follow it up with an increase on the opposite side.

It is important to keep the increases twisted — whether or not you are twisting your stitches, a twisted increase stitch will both hide its presence well, as well as help to hold together the stitch you increased into. This is espe-cially important with double increases.

Increases, like decreases, have a directional component that is used in decorative double-knitting. Instead of slanting, however, they're distinguished by the side of the pair the increase is on. A left-side increase is done on the left side of the pair being increased into; a right-side increase is done on the right side. A double increase (there is only one type, unlike with decreases) is done to both sides of the same pair.

Because of the directional nature of knitting — followed right to left — a right-side increase is done before the pair being increased into is made; a left-side increase is done after. A double increase is simply a right-side in-crease, a pair, and then a left-side increase.

There are other types of increases — the most common being the type where you use the bar between stitches to create a new stitch — but I find increases where a hole is created are not conducive to clean double-knitting work. It's probably best to keep those for lace and openwork.

RIGHT-SIDE INCREASE

Untwisted

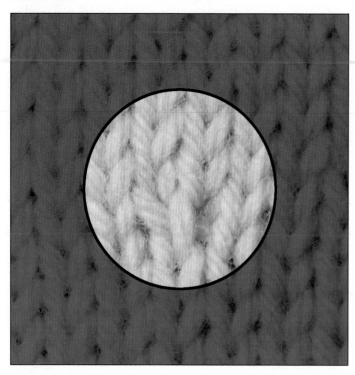

Twisted

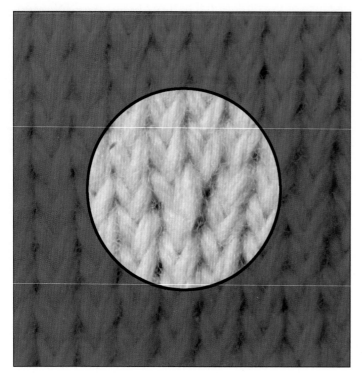

Facing side:

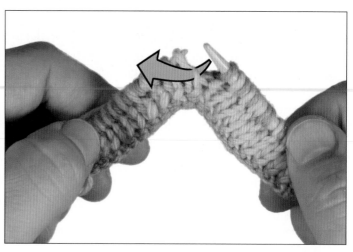

1) With both ends in back, insert the tip of the right needle into the stitch below the next stitch on your left needle, from back to front.

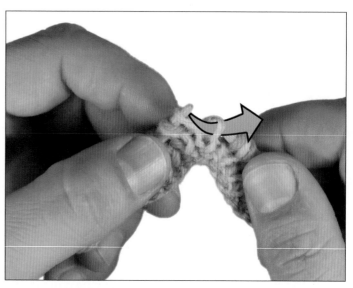

2) Put the picked-up stitch on your left needle, but don't remove the right needle. Keep the left needle in front.

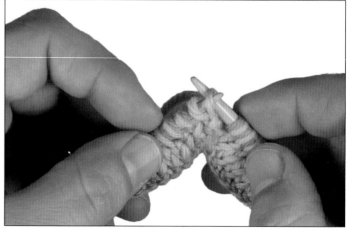

3) Knit with the color indicated by the pattern (K1TBL).

4) The increase looks like this on the facing side. Bring both ends to the front.

Opposite side:

5) Insert the tip of the right needle into the stitch below the next purl stitch on the left needle, from front to back. You may need to flip up your work a bit (as shown) to see what you're doing.

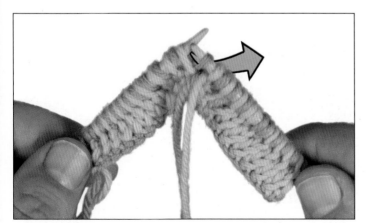

6) Put the picked-up stitch on the left needle, but don't remove the right needle. Keep the left needle in back.

7) Purl with the color indicated by the pattern.

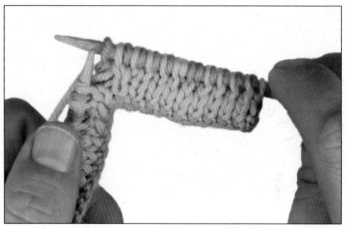

8) Bring both ends to the back. Work the next pair (the pair above the one you just increased into) as normal, in the colors indicated by the pattern. This shows the facing side with the increase done ...

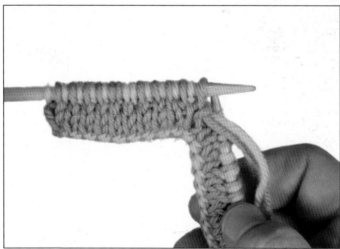

9) ... and this is the opposite side.

LEFT-SIDE INCREASE

Untwisted

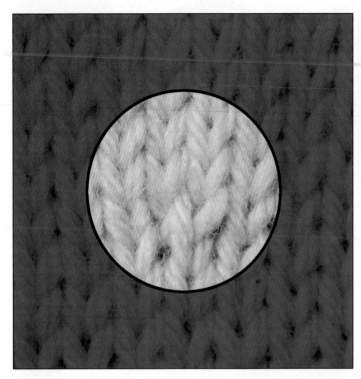

Twisted

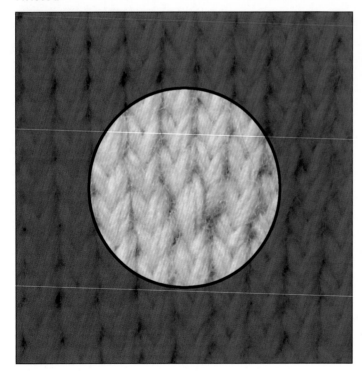

Facing side:

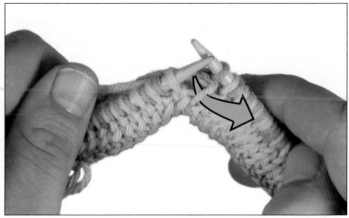

1) First, work the pair as normal in the colors indicated by the pattern. Then, with both ends in back, insert the tip of the left needle into the stitch two below the most recent knit stitch on the right needle, from back to front.

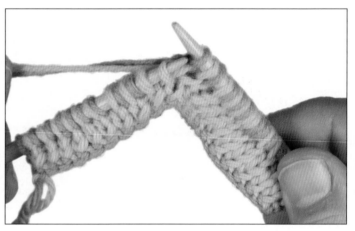

2) Leave the picked-up stitch on the left needle.

3) Knit the picked-up stitch with the color indicated by the pattern.

Opposite side:

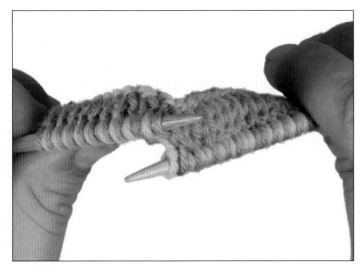

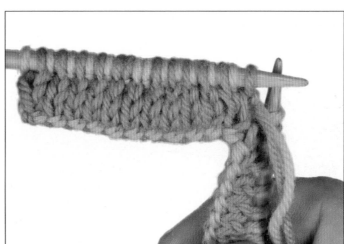

7) … and on the opposite side.

4) Bring both ends to the front. Insert the tip of the left needle into the stitch two below the most recent purl stitch on the right needle, from front to back. You may need to flip your work up a bit (as shown) to see what you're doing.

5) Purl through the back loop with the color indicated by the pattern (P1TBL)

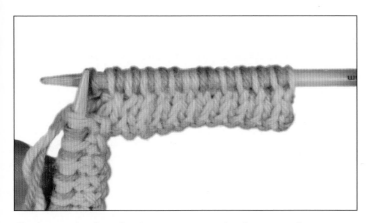

6) This is the finished increase on the facing side …

DOUBLE INCREASES

Untwisted

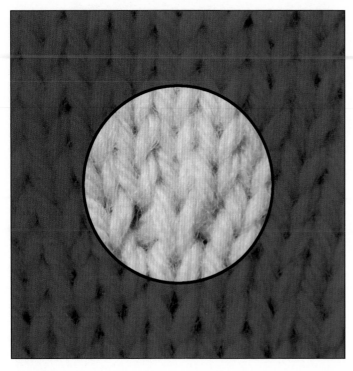

Twisted

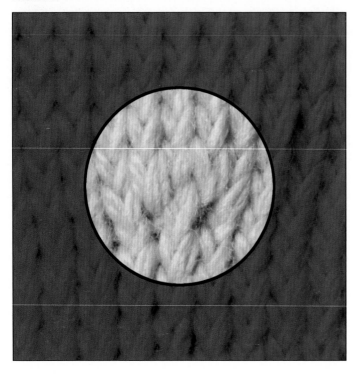

As it sounds, this is the increase complement to the double decrease. Rather than making one pair out of three, this makes three pairs out of one, by increasing into the right side and the left side of the same stitch. It is a centered technique.

1) Follow steps 1-7 in the right-side increase section above

2) Follow steps 1-5 in the left-side increase section above.

FOLLOWING INCREASES IN DOUBLE-KNITTING CHARTS

Increases in charts where they are used decoratively require slightly more thought. Because the chart element is only one pixel wide, but the increase creates either 1 or 2 extra stitches, you will need to pay attention not only to the element itself but to its surroundings.

 Right-side increase

 Left-side increase

Depicted above are the chart elements for a right-side increase and a left-side increase. In each, the vertical line represents the stitch the element is placed on, and the diagonal line represents the side the increase will be generated from. The pixel directly to the right of a right-side increase or to the left of a left-side increase is the color of the facing-side stitch of the pair you will be creating on that side; the opposite color will be used for the opposite-side stitch unless otherwise indicated.

 Double-increase

This is the chart element for a double-increase. Like the single increase, the vertical line represents the stitch the element is placed on, but in this case the diagonal lines point in both directions. The pixels directly to the left and right of a double increase are the colors of the facing-side stitches of the pairs generated by each directional increase; the opposite color will be used for the opposite-side stitches unless otherwise indicated.

PATTERN: BRATACH

Sample Knit by Astra

This hat is a simple application of decorative increasing and decreasing in double-knitting. Six banners or flags in 3 different Celtic knot motifs run diagonally around this hat and up to a spiral at the crown. Sizing this hat is very easy — the banners stay the same, but you add more pairs between them if you need a larger size. The more pairs between the banners, the more dramatic the crown spiral becomes! Also, because of the increases and decreases done in every round, the stitches in the spaces between the banners seem to run nearly horizontal. This is an illusion, of course, but a great generator of double-takes when you show off your hat — at least to other knitters. The crenellated brim is a function of the increases and decreases, and also becomes more dramatic the more pairs are inserted between the banners.

The word "bratach" means "flag" in Gaelic. I highly recommend you search out Mouth Music's first album for the song "Bratach Bana" or "white flags". True Scots may find the version a little untraditional, but I'll never forget my reaction to it when I heard it as a child.

MATERIALS:

[Color A] Queensland Collection Rustic Tweed (63%Wool, 27%Alpaca, 7% Acrylic, 3% Viscose); 278 yds/100g skein; #901: Natural; 1 skeins. 9 wpi.
[Color B] Queensland Collection Rustic Tweed (63%Wool, 27%Alpaca, 7% Acrylic, 3% Viscose); 278 yds/100g skein; #915: Purple; 1 skein. 9 wpi.

1 16-inch US5/3.75mm circular needle, or needle size required to achieve gauge desired.
1 set US5/3.75mm DPNs, or size to match circular needle above.
Tapestry needle.

GAUGE:

24 sts/28 rows = 4" in double-stockinette fabric.

SPECIAL TECHNIQUES

 Shift 1 left:

This is a combined right-side increase and left-slanting decrease. Using the increase and decrease instructions on pages 68 and 56 respectively, work up to (but don't yet work) the pair indicated by the pixel before the one this chart element is on. Make a right-side increase pair in the color configuration indicated by the pixel immediately to the right of the chart element, but instead of completing the increase by working the next pair, reorder the stitches of the next two pairs and work a left-slanting decrease in the color configuration indicated by the chart. This will keep the same number of pairs on the needles, but will "shift" a single pair to the left. It's a little like a mock cable technique.

When working this technique in this pattern, you will be increasing into stitches that had previously been decreases rather than regular pairs. It is important that you remember only to increase into the stitches on top of the decrease — i.e. the stitches that previously comprised the next pair — and not to pull the increased stitches through both stitches involved in the decrease.

PATTERN NOTES AND IDEAS

If you want to make the hat longer, Charts 2-4 all include at least one repeat of their individual pattern, so you can extrapolate extra rows to add to the bottom by copying them from later in the pattern. If you want it shorter, just start further up the pattern. Chart 1 acts as an end-cap, so it'll stay the same regardless of where you start in the next series of charts.

Don't add more to the top! The top of Charts 2-4 have to stay the same because they move right into Chart 5, which is the same for all 3 variations. If you add to the top, the pattern won't continue properly or you'll have to keep track of your own chart during the decreases. It's much easier to add more to the beginning, although it requires more forethought.

PATTERN

This chart uses 3 different Celtic knot motifs in varying complexity and length of repeat. They all start at different points in their respective repeat cycles, but end the same way once the decreases start.

First, you need to choose your size. If your gauge is 6 sts/in, then the six 10-pair cable motifs will give you a tube 10" around. Measure your head and subtract 10". The number of inches left is the number of pairs that need to be placed between each cable motif. For example, if your head is 22" around, 22 - 10 = 12. Put 12 pairs with the background color configuration between the cable motifs. If your head is 24" around, put 14 pairs between the cable motifs. If your gauge is 6 sts/in, every inch added to the circumference of this hat is one more pair added to each of the 6 spaces between the motifs.

Now, take the number you figured out above, add 10 and multiply by 6. This is the number you'll cast on.

Assuming a 6 sts/in gauge: For a 20 (22, 24)-inch hat, with Color A as FC and Color B as TC, cast on 120 (132, 144) pairs, or 240 (264, 288) individual stitches, using the standard double-knit cast-on method.

Work the foundation round: repeat Chart 1 twice, adding in your specified number of pairs between the motifs. Make sure that the pairs you add are worked with Color A as knit and Color B as purl.

Begin working Charts 2-4 in sequence. I've positioned them backwards on the page so they're more naturally placed, given that you'll be knitting right to left. The first pair in each chart is a right-side increase, so the motif shows the front color of the increased pair. Note that the column numbers start from the "second" pair in the chart — this is because the "first" pair is an increase off of the "second" pair. The last pair in each chart is a left-slanting decrease. The effect of this is to add a pair to one side and subtract a pair from the other side of each row of each motif — 6 increases and 6 decreases in every round. When a round is completed, the total number of pairs remains the same. The visual effect is that the cable motifs appear to slant at a 45-degree angle as they move up the body of the hat.

Repeat Chart 5 six times around the hat, switching to DPNs when necessary. Chart 5 is written for the 24" size but you don't have to follow the whole thing. If you need to size it larger than 24", the pattern is easily extrapolated larger by repeating the process you have been using

to shift and decrease, until there are 18 pairs left on the needles.

Work Chart 6. At this point there are no more increases, and the hat is finally ready to be cinched off. There should be 12 pairs left on the needles.

Cinch the top and weave in the ends as described in the Finishing section (page 158). You may want to block this pattern as the increases and decreases tend to make the fabric bunch a bit in certain areas. A little light steaming and ironing works wonders, however.

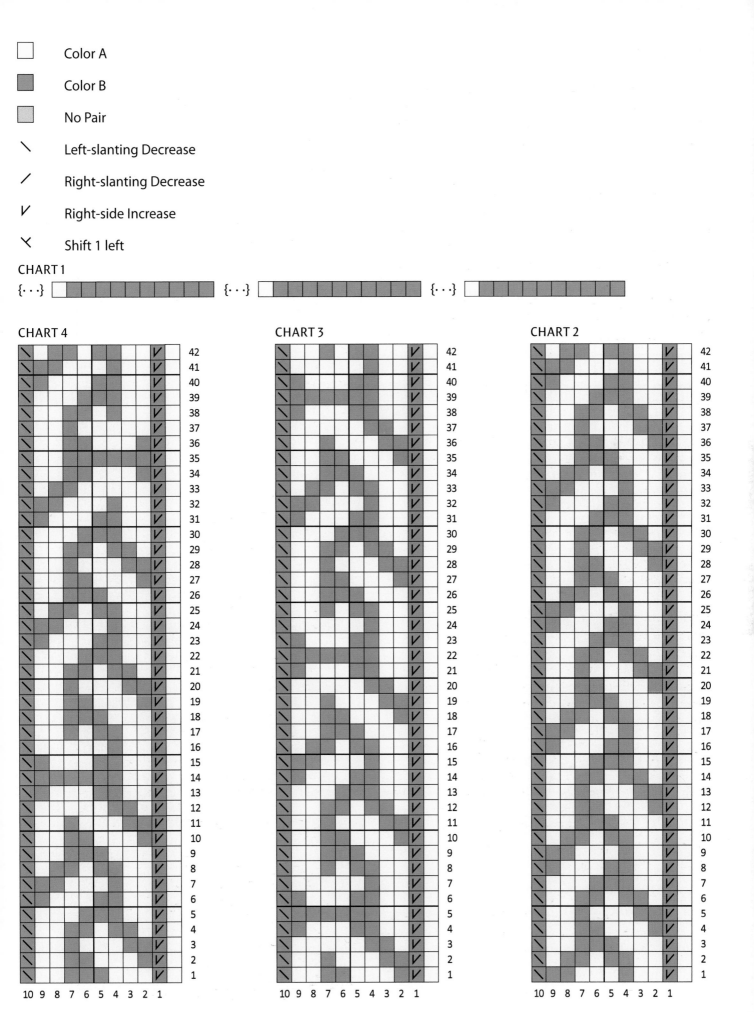

Color A

Color B

No Pair

\ Left-slanting Decrease

/ Right-slanting Decrease

V Right-side Increase

X Shift 1 left

CHART 1

CHART 4

CHART 3

CHART 2

CHART 5

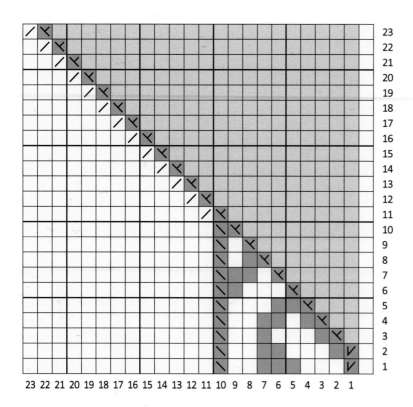

CHART 6

12 11 10 9 8 7 6 5 4 3 2 1

PATTERN: SILK CITY

Sample knit by Alasdair Post-Quinn

While thinking about what kinds of objects could really benefit from colorwork in double-knitting, I came up with the usual suspects: hats, scarves, blankets, maybe cuffs on sweaters — the list was really pretty short. I felt there must be more — and it occurred to me I hadn't seen many good necktie patterns in general. Those I had seen were either done in garter stitch — reversible by nature, but not terribly interesting — or required construction tantamount to actually sewing a tie out of fabric. Double-knitting seemed to me to be a perfect solution — it's reversible, it never curls, and it's easy to shape. Because a tie needs to be made out of thin enough fabric to make a rather large knot without being too bulky, it's best done in a finer-weight yarn — so I had the opportunity to chart a more detailed design.

MATERIALS:

[Color A] Crystal Palace Panda Silk fingering (52% bamboo; 43% machine washable Merino wool; 5% combed silk); 204 yds/50g skein; #3001: Pearl Blue; 1 skein. 14 wpi.
[Color B] Crystal Palace Panda Silk fingering (52% bamboo; 43% machine washable Merino wool; 5% combed silk); 204 yds/50g skein; #3013: Cocoa; 1 skein. 14 wpi.

1 set US2/2.75mm straight needles, or needle size required to achieve gauge.
Tapestry needle

GAUGE:

29 sts/38 rows = 4" in double-stockinette fabric. This tie is expected to be 3.75" wide at its widest point.

PATTERN NOTES AND IDEAS:

As the charts move forward, not every odd-numbered row is necessarily a facing-side row. On charts 3, 4 and 5, the odd-numbered rows are opposite-side rows. For all of the others, the odd-numbered rows are facing-side rows as usual.

The tie form set out here can easily be filled in with any pattern you like. Go to town with it!

PATTERN:

Using the standard double-knit cast-on, with Color B as FC and Color A as TC, cast on 1 pair, leaving approximately 4" of tail for weaving in. Turn and follow charts 1-5 in sequence. Follow Chart 6a-6b (Chart 6 is split in half because of the abnormally long repeat) 4 times. Follow Chart 7.. You should have one pair left on your needle when the final double-decrease is done. Break your ends, feed them through this last pair and tighten. Weave in ends from both tips of the tie.

☐	Color A
■	Color B
☐	No Pair
◖	Selvedge at end of facing-side row
◗	Selvedge at end of opposite-side row
⋁	Double-Increase
⋁	Right-side Increase
⋋	Left-side Increase
⟍	Left-slanting Decrease
⟋	Right-slanting Decrease
⋀	Standard Double-Decrease

CHART 1

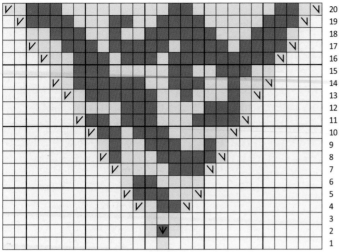

CHART 2

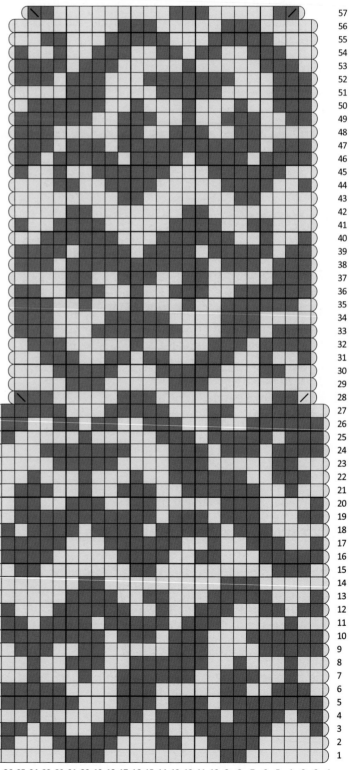

CHART 3

CHART 4

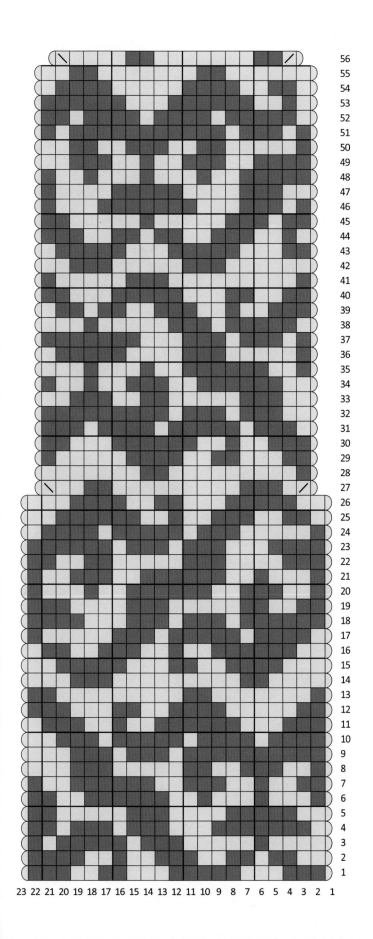

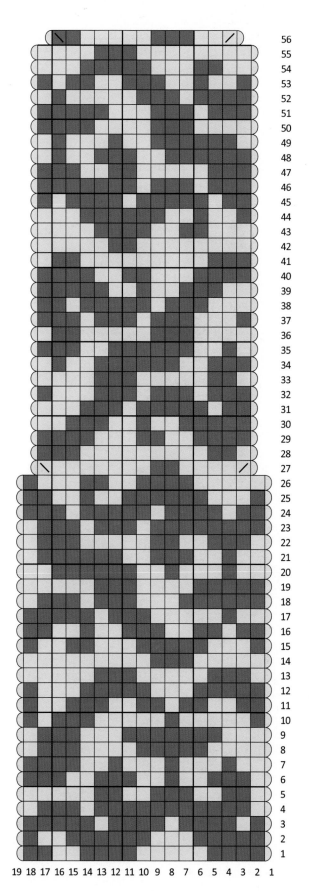

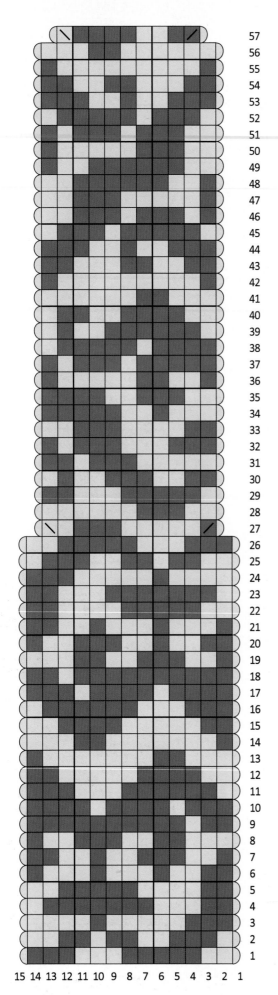

57
56
55
54
53
52
51
50
49
48
47
46
45
44
43
42
41
40
39
38
37
36
35
34
33
32
31
30
29
28
27
26
25
24
23
22
21
20
19
18
17
16
15
14
13
12
11
10
9
8
7
6
5
4
3
2
1

15 14 13 12 11 10 9 8 7 6 5 4 3 2 1

CHART 5
(LEFT)

CHART 6a
(RIGHT)

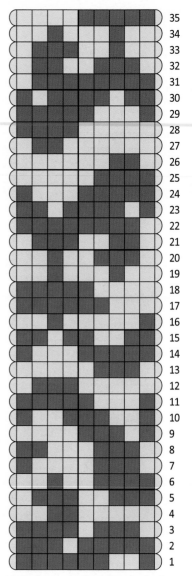

35
34
33
32
31
30
29
28
27
26
25
24
23
22
21
20
19
18
17
16
15
14
13
12
11
10
9
8
7
6
5
4
3
2
1

11 10 9 8 7 6 5 4 3 2 1

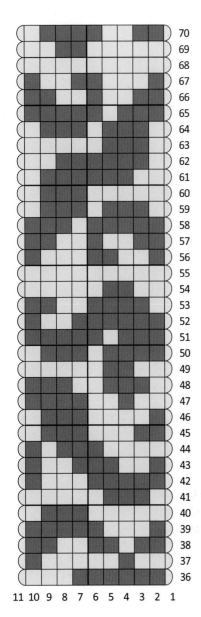

70
69
68
67
66
65
64
63
62
61
60
59
58
57
56
55
54
53
52
51
50
49
48
47
46
45
44
43
42
41
40
39
38
37
36

11 10 9 8 7 6 5 4 3 2 1

CHART 6b
(LEFT)

CHART 7
(RIGHT)

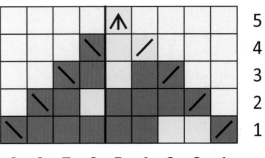

5
4
3
2
1

9 8 7 6 5 4 3 2 1

PATTERN: SILK ROAD

Sample knit by Alasdair Post-Quinn

This necktie is, quite frankly, utter insanity. I will admit without reservation that this pattern was the one piece I was not confident I would be able to design properly. It's an optical illusion — what appear to be lots of interlinked spirals are in fact just segments of zigzag patterns offset horizontally by one pair. I'd like to thank Kieran Foley for sowing the seeds that helped my brain grow this fruit. Many people have told me that the resulting pattern almost doesn't look as if it was knitted at all.

MATERIALS:

[Color A] Crystal Palace Panda Silk fingering (52% bamboo; 43% machine washable Merino wool; 5% combed silk); 204 yds/50g skein; #3002: Butterscotch; 1 skein. 14 wpi.

[Color B] Crystal Palace Panda Silk fingering(52% bamboo; 43% machine washable Merino wool; 5% combed silk); 204 yds/50g skein; #3011: Sangria; 1 skein. 14 wpi.

1 set US2/2.75mm straight needles, or needle size required to achieve gauge.
Tapestry needle

GAUGE:

29 sts/38 rows = 4" in double-stockinette fabric. However, since this is not double-stockinette fabric, expect about a 10% decrease in width from the expected stitch gauge. This tie is expected to be 3.25" wide at its widest point.

SPECIAL TECHNIQUES:

Double-decrease/left-side increase: This is what happens when two increase/decrease techniques get too close together — they fuse into one.

Referring to the double-decrease and increase techniques on pages 60 and 70 respectively, work the double-decrease as normal in the color configuration indicated by the chart. Then, before working the next pair, increase into the left side of the decrease. Make sure to only pick up the stitches that comprised the previous pair — don't pull the increased stitches through more than one stitch in the decrease.

PATTERN NOTES AND IDEAS:

This spiral pattern was generated by taking two expanses of horizontal zigzag patterns — made up of increases and decreases built into a mock-ribbing pattern — and shifting them one pair off center from one another. Experiment with this! Try spacing the increase and decrease columns further apart; make the horizontal section taller before shifting; try shifting two or three pairs off center, perhaps in the opposite direction, and see how the pattern changes. It's a fascinating technique. It also works well in stranded knitting, to save time while experimenting with shapes.

PATTERN:

Using the standard double-knit cast-on, with Color A as FC and Color B as TC, cast on 1 pair, leaving approximately 4" of tail for weaving in. Turn and follow charts 1-5 in sequence. Follow Chart 6 seven times. Follow Chart 7. You should have one pair left on your needle when the final double-decrease is done. Break your ends, feed them through this last pair and tighten. Weave in ends from both tips of the tie.

CHART 1

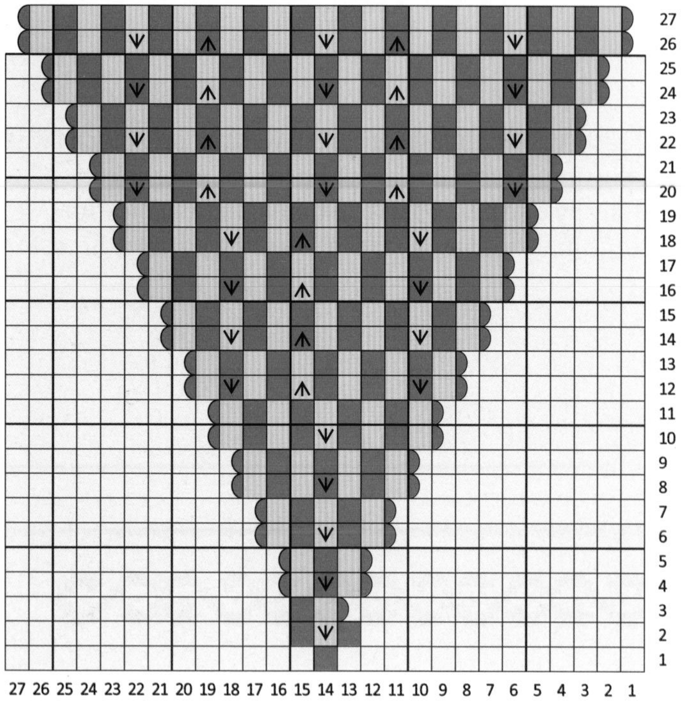

CHART 2

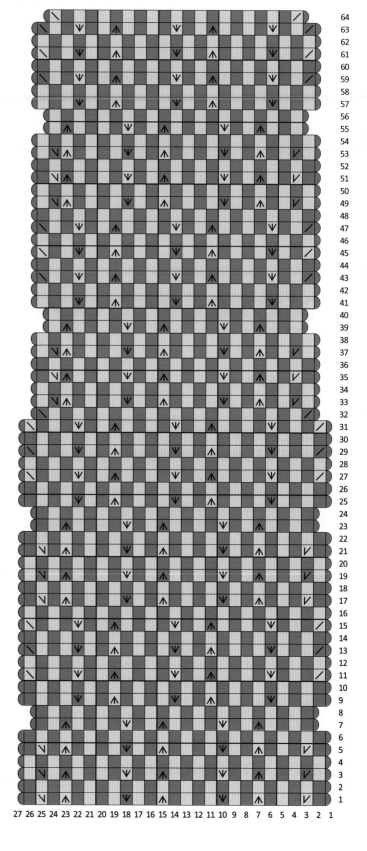

Color A

Color B

No Pair

Selvedge at end of facing-side row

Selvedge at end of opposite-side row

∨ Double-Increase

∧ Standard Double-Decrease

V Right-side Increase

⟍ Left-side Increase

╲ Left-slanting Decrease

╱ Right-slanting Decrease

⋏ Double-Decrease/Left-side Increase

CHART 3

CHART 4

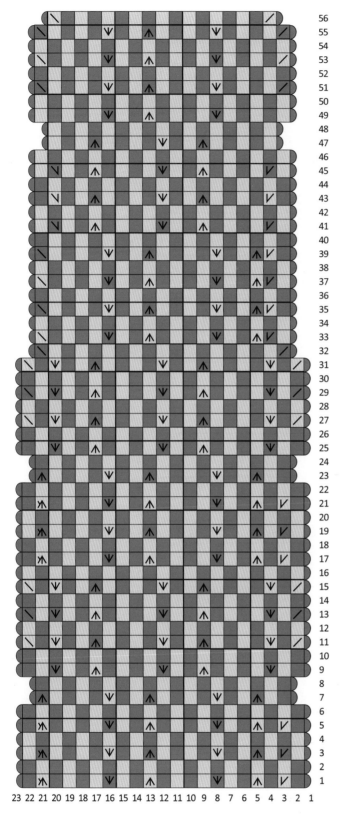

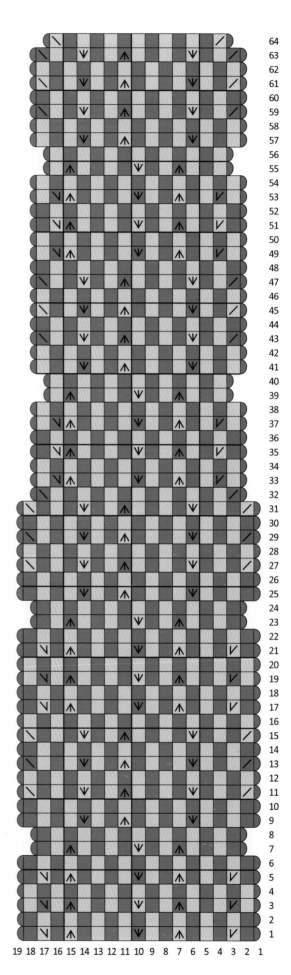

CHART 5

CHART 6

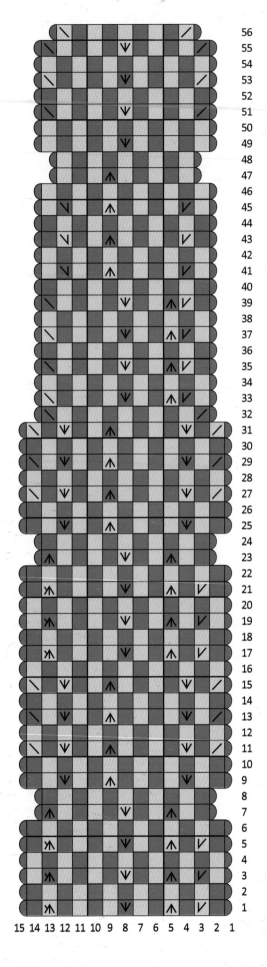

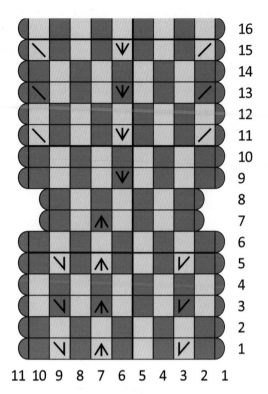

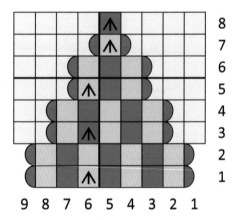

CHAPTER 4: TWO-PATTERN DOUBLE-KNITTING

Okay, now that you have the rules of double-knitting well and truly learned, it's time to break one.

So far, you have done double-knitting with the same pattern on both sides — reversed in color and orientation, but essentially the same. However, what if you wanted to do something with a different chart on either side?

Letters in particular have been troublesome for double-knitters — because the opposite side shows the mirror image of the facing side, many letters of the alphabet are unreadable on one side of standard double-knitting. I stumbled across a way of working the two faces in different patterns after making a mistake and working both the knit and the purl stitch of a particular pair in the same color. I was surprised to find that this can be done, to some degree, in double-knit fabric. You can't make both sides the same color — you would end up with 1x1 ribbing — but you can make some pairs all Color A, and some all Color B. If it is possible to make one pair not follow the rule of reversing colors, it is possible to use this technique to work two patterns, one on each side.

Originally, I called this technique "non-reversible" double-knitting. The name didn't sit well with me, since the fabric was still reversible. If anything, it was more reversible. I suppose it could have been called "super-reversible" but I settled on the more descriptive "two-pattern" double-knitting.

The difficulty with this new method lay in the charting. Normal double-knitting charts are the same as any other colorwork chart; the knitter has to infer the opposite side. But when the opposite side is not easily inferred from the content of the facing side, a new notation must be developed.

I decided to go with a literal approach. In order to knit two patterns at the same time, you alternate columns of the two patterns and knit and purl the individual stitches in the colors the chart calls for. The pairs are still treated the same — the facing-side stitch is still knit with both ends in back; the opposite-side stitch is still purled with both ends in front — but the rule about always purling the opposite color from the knitted color in each pair can be broken if two patterns are desired.

In truth, this technique may be easier to do than standard double-knitting. Rather than having only half the chart in front of you at any given time, two-pattern double-knitting uses a chart that is completely literal. The difficulty is in creating that chart to begin with. Once the chart is planned and generated, the knitting is just a matter of keeping a careful eye on the chart.

The generation of these charts is easiest if you do your charting with a computer, but can be done "longhand" if need be. Here are the steps to follow, assuming your chart is a letter that needs to be readable on both sides:

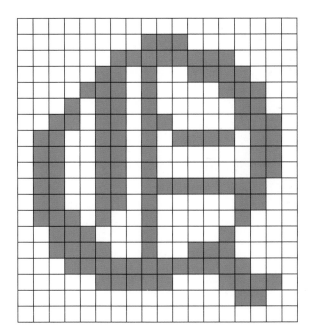

1) Chart out your letter. Here, I'm using a capital Q in an Old-English font.

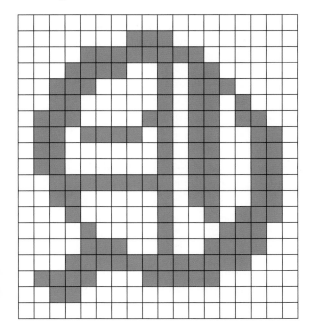

2) Make a second copy with the colors reversed.

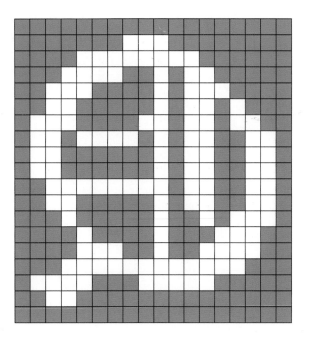

3) Make a mirror-image copy — if using a software program, reflect on a vertical axis.

4) Overlay the mirror-image pattern with purl dots.

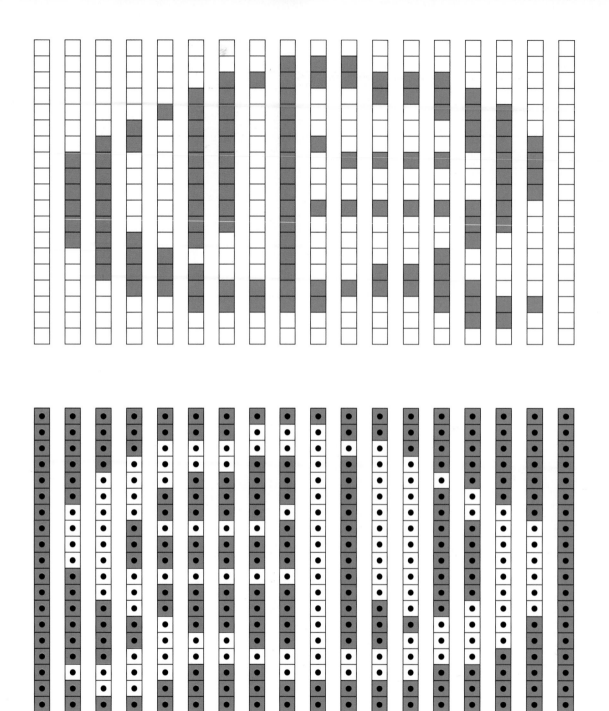

5) Separate all the columns of both patterns by one column.

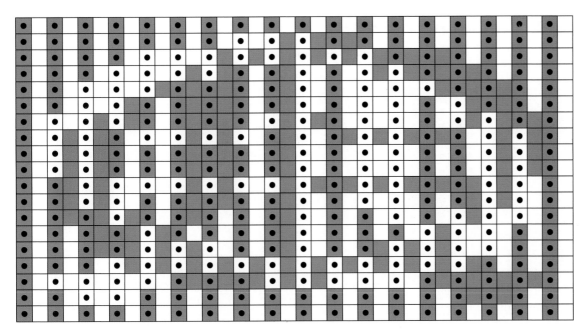

6) Interlace the resulting charts so that the first column is from the knitted pattern and the last column is from the purled pattern (right to left, as normally followed).

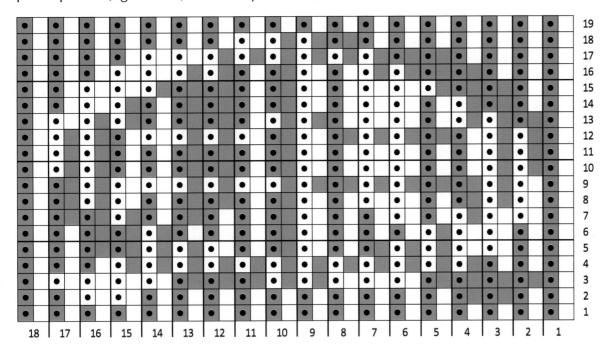

7) Add your row and column numbers, and grid lines if you choose. I add horizontal grid lines every 5 rows, and vertical grid lines in between every pair, extending from the bottom a little to make it clear where the pairs are. It can get confusing otherwise.

You are welcome to work up the chart in Step 7 above to get a feel for how this works. Following these charts in the round is easier than in the flat — in flat two-pattern double-knitting, the opposite side row reverses symbols while keeping the same colors. You can ignore the knit and purl symbols if you just remember that the rule about which stitch in a pair is knitted and which is purled still applies regardless of which side you are working on.

The same planning method also works if you want to chart two different motifs, or even for all-over patterns, if their repeats are the same (or at least have a common denominator). It is best for the opposite-side chart (the one overlaid with purl dots) to have the opposite background color from the facing side; otherwise the background sections will become 1x1 ribbing.

EXERCISE: ALGIERS/FLOWER CHART

To get a feel for the technique, give this exercise a try:

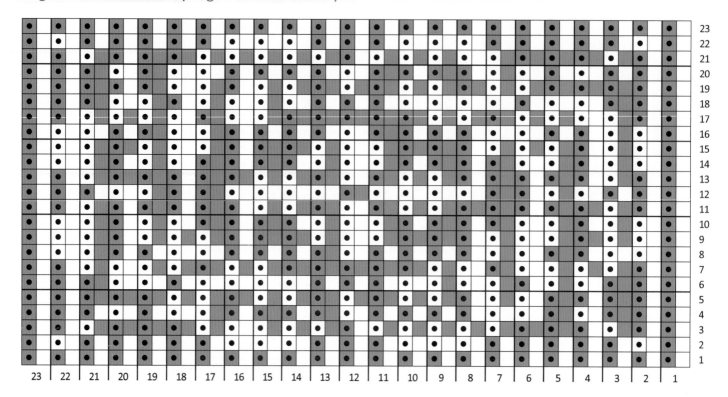

Choose two well-contrasting colors in a DK or worsted-weight plain yarn and appropriately-sized needles. Designate the lighter of the two colors as "Color A" and the darker as "Color B". If the two colors contrast well but neither is clearly lighter than the other, the designation is arbitrary, so just stay consistent.

Using Color B as the FC and Color A as the TC, cast on 23 pairs or 46 total stitches using the standard double-knit cast-on.

Follow the chart. The first and last pairs in the chart are plain double-stockinette with no color changes, so you can use the selvedge if you like.

Bind off with the standard double-knit bind-off.

I will leave the patterns on the facing and opposite sides as a pleasant surprise. Normally, when I do a two-pattern chart, I like to have a small "thumbnail" image of what each side is going to look like, to give the knitter a clear image to check his or her work against. You will see this in the various patterns which use this technique.

PATTERN: OPEN FOR BUSINESS

Sample knit by Marialyce Weideman

This was a concept I had a while ago, after discovering the wonder of two-pattern double-knitting. There were some logistical issues to work out, though, before I could finally complete the design. It was important to me that the work be of a high resolution — in other words, smaller yarn. I scrounged around for good letter charts before I finally just decided to make my own from scratch. I also needed to figure out how to get the sign to stay flat rather than flopping around as fabric is usually wont to do. I toyed with stretching it on a frame, but decided instead on the more elegant solution documented here. You are of course welcome to mount it however you like.

MATERIALS:

[Color A] Harrisville Designs New England Shetland (100% wool); 217 yds/50g skein; #46: Oatmeal; 1 skein. 14 wpi.
[Color B] Harrisville Designs New England Shetland (100% wool); 217 yds/50g skein; #36: Garnet; 1 skein. 14 wpi.

1 US2/2.75mm 20" circular needle, or needle size required to achieve gauge
2 wire coat hangers
Wire cutter
Tapestry needle

GAUGE:

23 sts/29 rows = 4" in double-stockinette fabric after blocking. Because this item is not sized, gauge is not critical. The sample is 18.5" wide when blocked.

PATTERN NOTES AND IDEAS:

If you're going to be hanging this in the sun, keep in mind that sun will bleach most dyed yarns. It may be worth considering natural fiber colors (mostly browns and blacks to grays and whites), or hanging it somewhere still visible but out of the sun.

PATTERN:

In this pattern, the odd-numbered rows are opposite-side rows. This means that the first row you do will be an opposite-side row. However, you will be matching the colors of your cast-on pairs, so that shouldn't pose much difficulty. The reason I do this is because the two-pattern work starts on an even-numbered row, and it's easier to start two-pattern work on a facing-side row.

Cast on 112 pairs or 224 total stitches, using the standard double-knitting cast-on with Color B as FC and Color A as TC. Turn and start the pattern in Chart 1 in standard double-knitting — keeping in mind that row 1 is an opposite-side row. Continue with Chart 2 and Chart 3. The entire piece consists of Charts 1, 2 and 3 lined up in a row. The full chart is split to fit on the page.

Make sure to leave the edges open as charted if you plan to use my permanent blocking method; if you plan to use your own mounting solution, you may leave the edges closed.

Inside the green box, the work switches from standard to two-pattern double-knitting. In Chart 1, follow the two-pattern Chart 1a inside this box; in Chart 2, follow Chart 2a inside the box; and in Chart 3, follow Chart 3a inside the box. Keep in mind that on opposite-side rows you will be following Charts 1a, 2a and 3a backwards — reversed in stitch type but true to the colors shown.

Once row 39 is done, bind off using the standard double-knitting bind-off, then tuck the ends into the hollow space along the top and bottom edges.

Block and mount, or use the permanent blocking method illustrated below.

PERMANENT BLOCKING

This is the reason for those color-changed borders, aside from the stylish look. As you've seen, standard double-knitting is hollow; whenever one color is used on one side and another is used on the other side consistently (i.e. for a large expanse), the two layers can be separated. A color change in a row locks the two layers together — however, a color change between rows will only be anchored at the edges. The color-changed borders create a narrow path all the way around the work, using the crenellations in rows 3 and 37 to lock the horizontal color change together.

We're going to make the piece structurally sound by inserting a pair of cleverly-bent coat hangers inside this pathway. You will need the type that's all wire and can be untwisted. Cut off the twisty bits and straighten the whole thing out as best you can. Stretch the work to the size you want it and measure one of the long edges. Find the middle of the coat hanger and figure half of the long edge measurement, then bend the hanger to a right angle at that point. Now measure the side edge. If the hanger measures longer than the side edge from the end to the bend, bend it again at a right angle so it will fit. Don't do this to the other side yet! Repeat with the second hanger.

Now, you're going to put the long end of one hanger into the top edge of the sign, from one side. Work the hanger carefully in, making sure to keep it between the layers. If the cut ends of the hanger are rough, you can use a metal file or put a bit of electrical tape around them before inserting them to keep them from catching on stray fibers.

Once the hanger is most of the way in, feed its short bent end into the bottom gusset. Once it's positioned, bend the other end of the hanger down, making sure the hanger will lay flat on a table. Again, bend the short piece at the bottom. Both bent ends of the hanger should be as close to symmetrical as possible, since the center of the hanger should be at the center of the top edge. You can let the hanger's bent short ends out of the bottom gusset while you repeat from bottom to top with the other hanger. Make sure all 4 short ends of the hanger fit into their respective pathways.

Now thread a tapestry needle with either color and seam the two edges together over the hanger, sealing the hanger inside. Use whichever seaming stitch you most prefer. Weave in the ends, straighten the work, and your permanent blocking is done. If it gets loose over time, you can unseam it and repeat the process with some new hangers.

Because there is a solid internal frame, you can hang the sign in whatever way strikes your fancy. It's easy to use a ribbon or another yarn to make a hanging cord, or you can stick it on a nail or a hook, right through the knitted fabric.

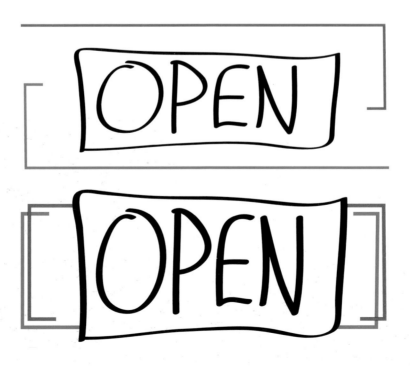

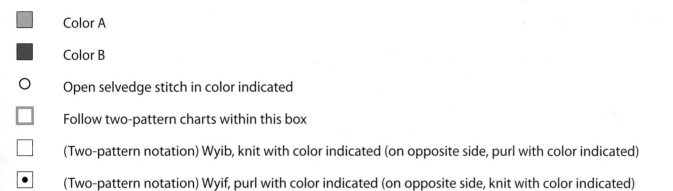

Color A

Color B

O   Open selvedge stitch in color indicated

☐   Follow two-pattern charts within this box

☐   (Two-pattern notation) Wyib, knit with color indicated (on opposite side, purl with color indicated)

[•]   (Two-pattern notation) Wyif, purl with color indicated (on opposite side, knit with color indicated)

CHART 1

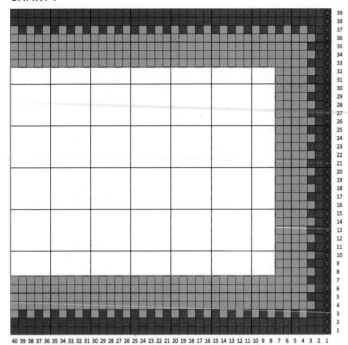

Row numbers (right side): 39 38 37 36 35 34 33 32 31 30 29 28 27 26 25 24 23 22 21 20 19 18 17 16 15 14 13 12 11 10 9 8 7 6 5 4 3 2 1

Column numbers (bottom): 40 39 38 37 36 35 34 33 32 31 30 29 28 27 26 25 24 23 22 21 20 19 18 17 16 15 14 13 12 11 10 9 8 7 6 5 4 3 2 1

CHART 3

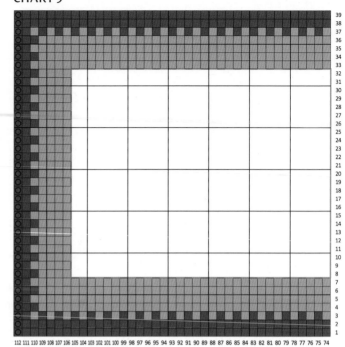

Row numbers (right side): 39 38 37 36 35 34 33 32 31 30 29 28 27 26 25 24 23 22 21 20 19 18 17 16 15 14 13 12 11 10 9 8 7 6 5 4 3 2 1

Column numbers (bottom): 112 111 110 109 108 107 106 105 104 103 102 101 100 99 98 97 96 95 94 93 92 91 90 89 88 87 86 85 84 83 82 81 80 79 78 77 76 75 74

CHART 2

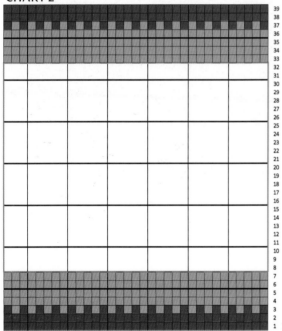

Row numbers (right side): 39 38 37 36 35 34 33 32 31 30 29 28 27 26 25 24 23 22 21 20 19 18 17 16 15 14 13 12 11 10 9 8 7 6 5 4 3 2 1

Column numbers (bottom): 73 72 71 70 69 68 67 66 65 64 63 62 61 60 59 58 57 56 55 54 53 52 51 50 49 48 47 46 45 44 43 42 41

CHART 1a

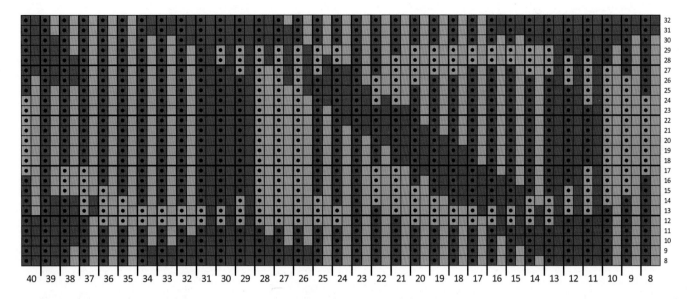

40 39 38 37 36 35 34 33 32 31 30 29 28 27 26 25 24 23 22 21 20 19 18 17 16 15 14 13 12 11 10 9 8

CHART 2a

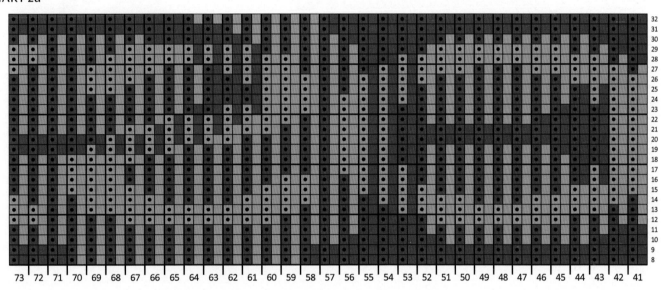

73 72 71 70 69 68 67 66 65 64 63 62 61 60 59 58 57 56 55 54 53 52 51 50 49 48 47 46 45 44 43 42 41

CHART 3a

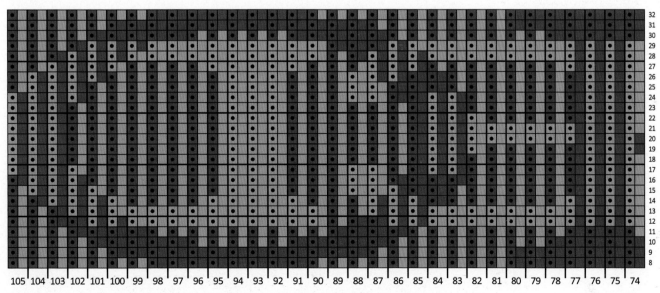

105 104 103 102 101 100 99 98 97 96 95 94 93 92 91 90 89 88 87 86 85 84 83 82 81 80 79 78 77 76 75 74

PATTERN: FOUR WINDS

Samples knit by Michelle Gibbs, Alasdair Post-Quinn

This hat was first published in the Winter 2009 issue of the online magazine Twist Collective. Since that publication, I have made a number of improvements to the pattern, including a new set of compass points which use decorative increasing and decreasing to achieve smooth-edged points rather than the jagged ones on the original version. The hat construction remains modular — there are two bands, two closures and now two sets of compass points charted, for a total of 8 possible hats. This is a refinement of my second effort at two-pattern double-knitting. The letter band is especially interesting, since the N and S are readable from both sides, but the E and the W actually switch places so that the compass is correct on both sides.

MATERIALS:

Nautical Blue colorway:

[Color A] Cascade 220 (100% wool); 220 yds/100g skein; #8010; 1 skein. 9 wpi.
[Color B] Cascade 220 (100% wool); 220 yds/100g skein; #8887; 1 skein. 9 wpi.

Parchment brown colorway

[Color A] Cascade 220 (100% wool); 220 yds/100g skein; #8021; 1 skein. 9 wpi.
[Color B] Cascade 220 (100% wool); 220 yds/100g skein; #2411; 1 skein. 9 wpi.

1 US6/4mm circular needle, or needle size required to achieve gauge desired.
1 set US6/4mm DPNs, or needle size to match circular needle above.
Tapestry needle

GAUGE:

20sts/27 rows = 4" in double-stockinette fabric.

PATTERN NOTES AND IDEAS:

I had a resident of New Orleans write to tell me that I'd put the fleur-de-lis pattern upside down, and it really ought to be right-side up! Actually, if you look at a compass, the fleur-de-lis points North — and if you look at this hat, the fleur-de-lis is pointing in the same direction as the North point — down. I realize I am being inconsistent — the letters are pointed in the correct direction for readability but the wrong direction for the compass. If you really want to make sure the fleur-de-lis points up, just flip the chart.

PATTERN:

Cast on 104 pairs or 208 individual stitches, using the cast-on method described on page 2. Because this hat cannot be sized up or down, it is up to your gauge to do that. I have found that Cascade 220 can effectively be knit on needles from US5 to US8. US5 needles should give you approximately a 19" hat; US6 needles should give you a 21" hat; and US7 should give you a 23" hat. Any further sizing will probably have to be done with a different yarn.

1) Choose a Band:

a. For Band 1, which is a standard double-knit pattern with a fleur-de-lis on the North point, diamonds on the other 3 cardinal directions and dots on the 4 semi-cardinal directions, work Chart 1a twice, Chart 1b once, then Chart 1a once.

b. For Band 2, which has two-pattern cardinal directions which are readable and orientable from either side, work Chart 2 four times around. Inside the green box, work the two-pattern Charts 2a-d in sequence.

2) Choose a Compass:

a. For Compass 1, which is a standard double-knit pattern, work Chart 3 four times around.

b. For Compass 2, which smoothes out the jagged edges of the points with some complex increasing and decreasing, work Chart 4 four times around.

3) Choose a Closure:

a. For Closure 1, which uses a pair of single-decreases next to each other, work Chart 5 four times around.

b. For Closure 2, which uses double-decreases, work Chart 6a once then Chart 6b three times.

Transfer the work to DPNs when necessary, and when done with the closure, cinch the top as described in the chapter on Finishing (page 158).

CHART 1a

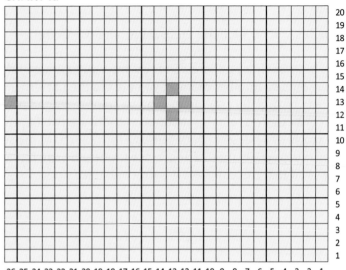

CHART 1b

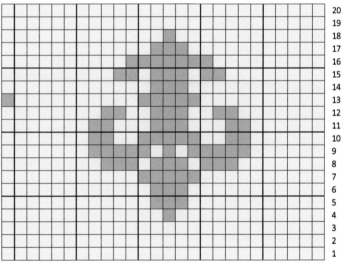

☐	Color A
▨	Color B
▨	No Pair
\	Left-slanting Decrease
/	Right-slanting Decrease
V	Right-side Increase
⅄	Left-side Increase
人	Ridged Double-Decrease
Λ	Standard Double-Decrease
V	Double-Increase
☐	Follow two-pattern charts within this box
☐	(Two-pattern notation) Wyib, knit with color indicated
☐•	(Two-pattern notation) Wyif, purl with color indicated

CHART 2

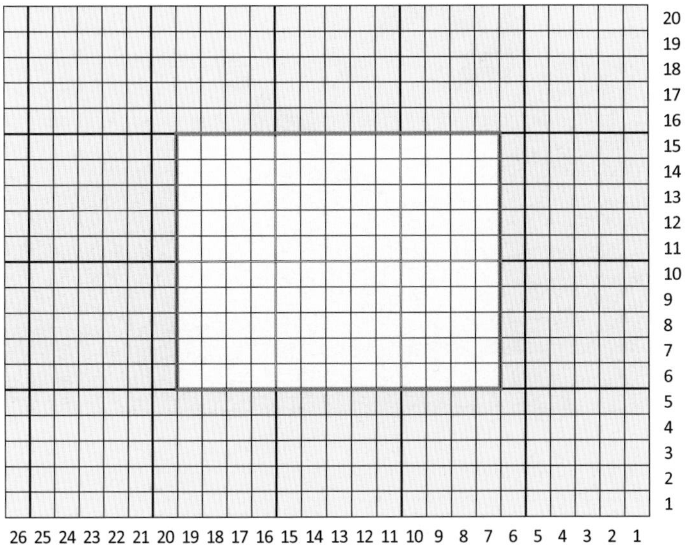

20 19 18 17 16 15 14 13 12 11 10 9 8 7 6 5 4 3 2 1

26 25 24 23 22 21 20 19 18 17 16 15 14 13 12 11 10 9 8 7 6 5 4 3 2 1

CHART 2a

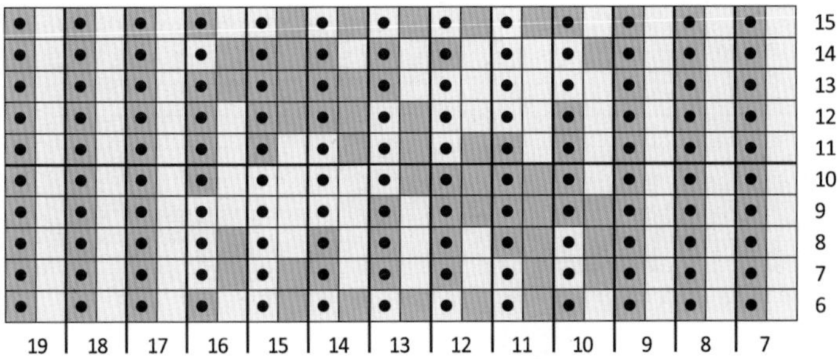

15 14 13 12 11 10 9 8 7 6

19 18 17 16 15 14 13 12 11 10 9 8 7

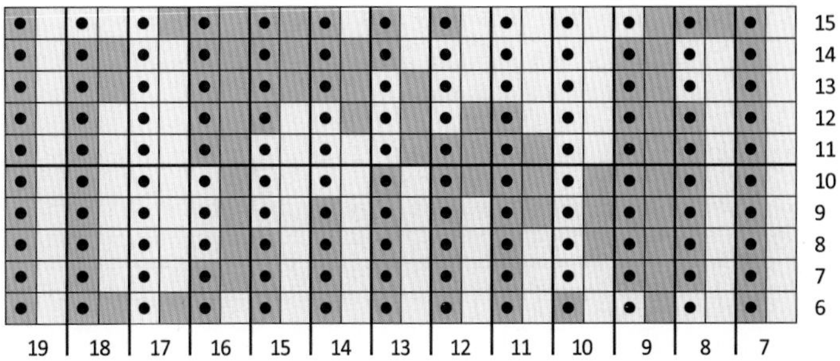

OUTSIDE 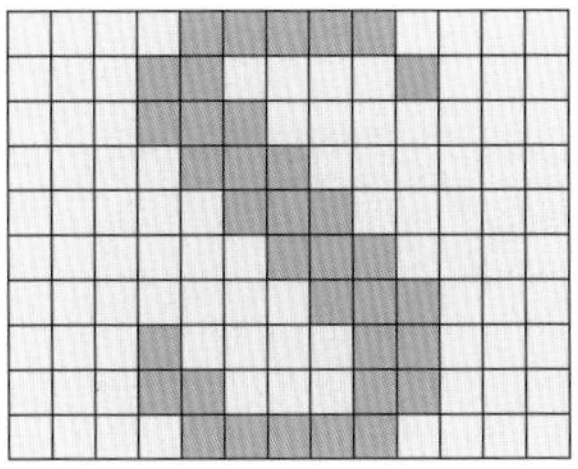   INSIDE

CHART 2c

15 14 13 12 11 10 9 8 7 6

19 18 17 16 15 14 13 12 11 10 9 8 7

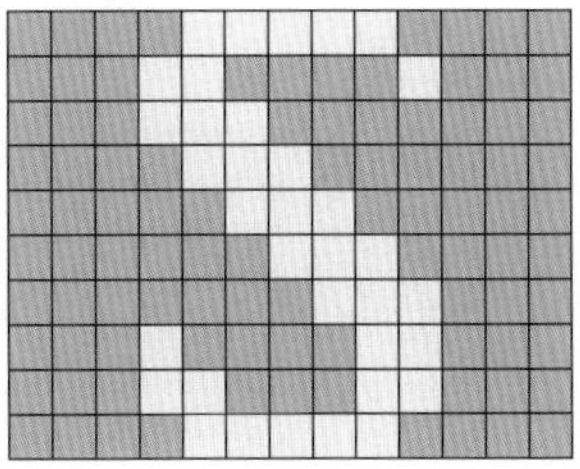

OUTSIDE 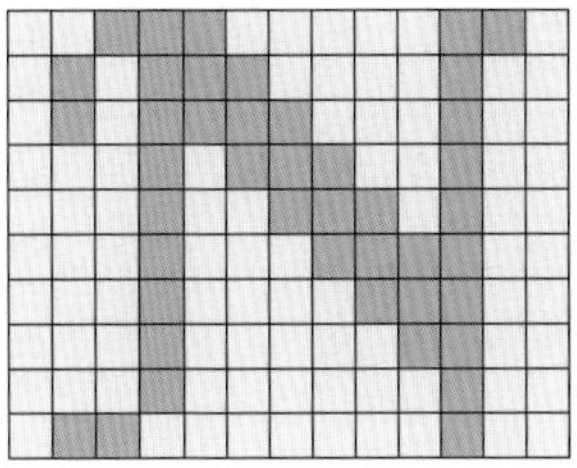   INSIDE

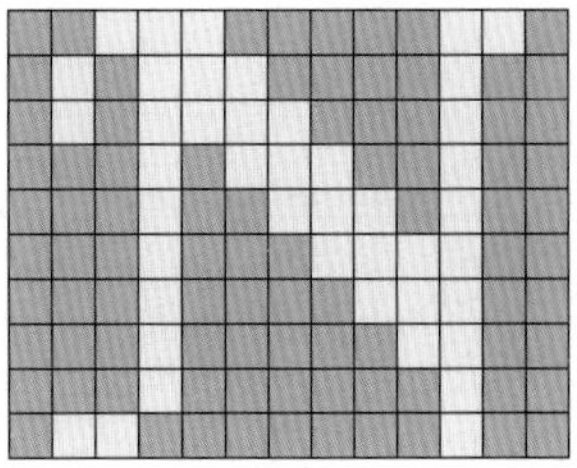

CHART 2b

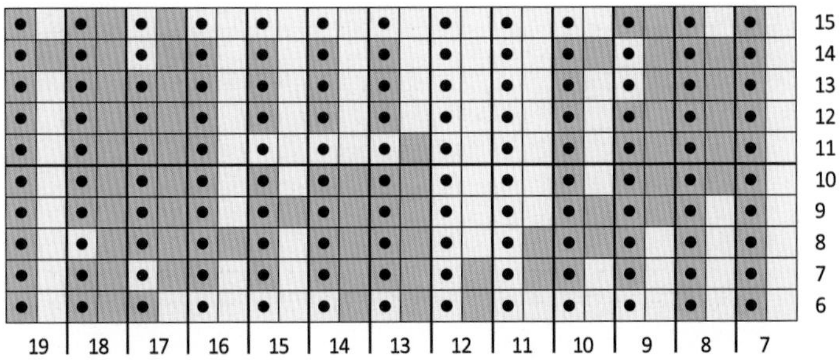

15 14 13 12 11 10 9 8 7 6

19 18 17 16 15 14 13 12 11 10 9 8 7

CHART 2d

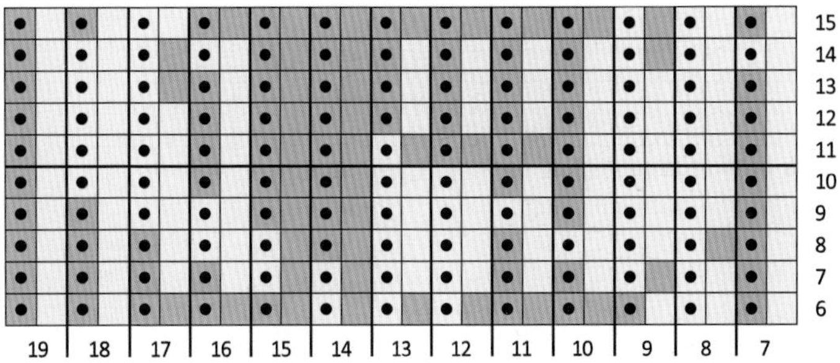

15 14 13 12 11 10 9 8 7 6

19 18 17 16 15 14 13 12 11 10 9 8 7

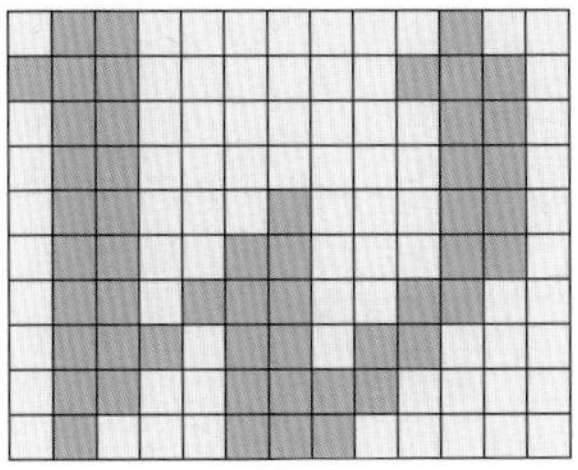

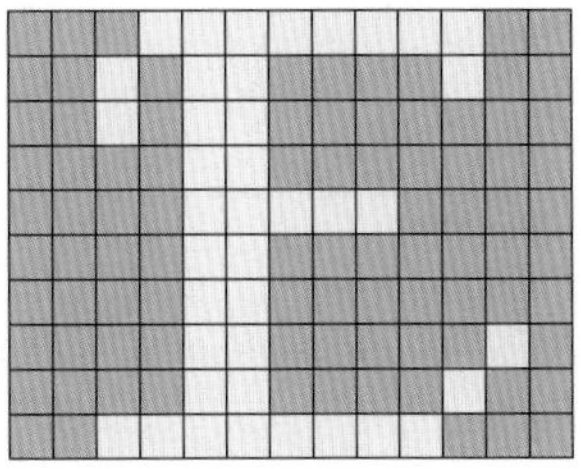

OUTSIDE 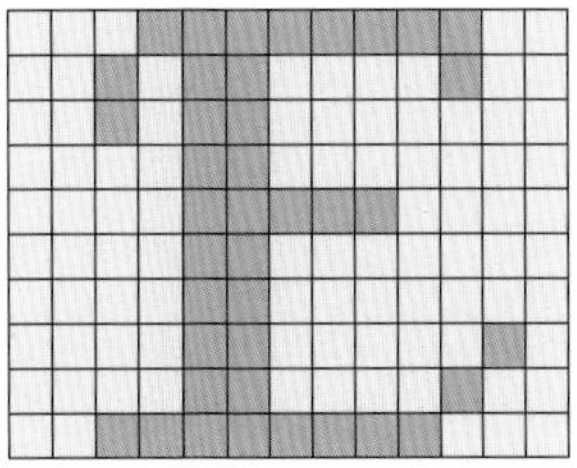   INSIDE

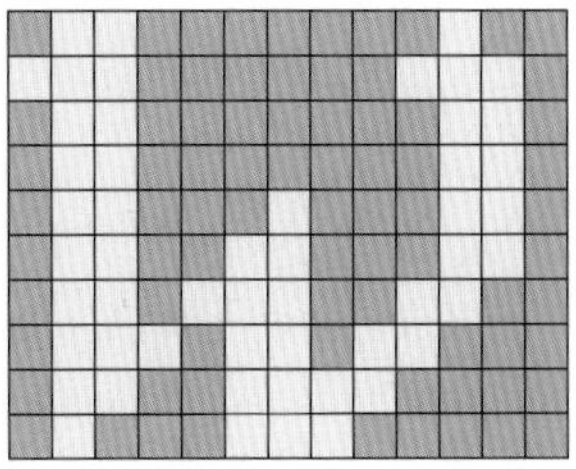

CHART 3

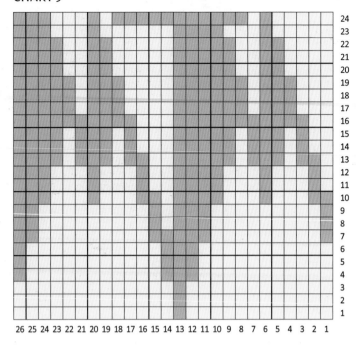

CHART 4

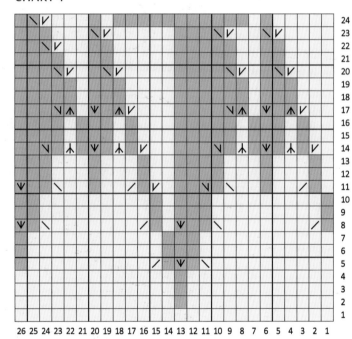

CHART 5

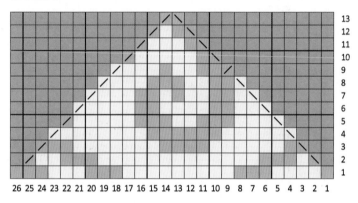

CHART 6a

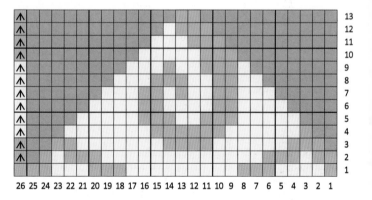

CHART 6b

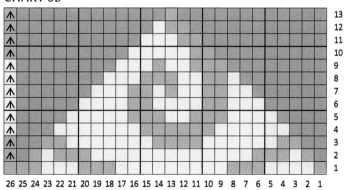

CHAPTER 5: MULTI-COLOR DOUBLE-KNITTING

Up until now, traditional double-knitting has been limited to two colors. Indeed, even stranded colorwork is usually limited to two colors per row or round, mostly because of the difficulty of managing three or more ends.

I struggled for a little while trying to think about how to add a third color to standard double-knitting. I called it "triple-knitting". Logic would seem to indicate that if a two-color double-knit piece has two sides, then a three-color piece must have three sides. Where does the third side go? Do we have to have triads on the needle now instead of pairs? Are we knitting into the fourth dimension here?

In reality, it's nothing so complex.

Multi-color double-knitting is actually done using the same pair structure as standard double-knitting. There are still only two faces, one knit and one purl per pair. However, if there are three ends, the unused color has to be hidden somewhere.

The structure of double-knitting comes into play here. If you remember from earlier in the book — and your own observations of double-knit fabric in the pieces you've already knit — there is a space inside each pair. The more pairs of the same color configuration in an area, the more likely you'll be able to actually separate the two sides of the fabric, but even a single pair alone in an expanse of the opposite color has a space between its knit and its purl. That space can be used to hide things like unused strands.

Therefore, three-color double-knitting is worked like this:

1) Cast on with two colors.

2) Add the third color before starting to work the first pair. Hold the third end together with the other two.

3) With ends in back, K1 in the color indicated by chart.

4) With ends in front, P1 in one of the other two colors.

The third color, if it is traveling with the other two, will naturally hide between the two layers.

COLOR MANAGEMENT IN MULTI-COLOR DOUBLE-KNITTING

In step 4 above, it says "P1 in one of the other two colors". How do you know which? In standard double-knitting, a motif on the opposite side is always reversed in color from the same motif on the facing side. But with three colors, "reversing" colors isn't an option. Instead, you have to rotate the colors. The key here is consistency. You can choose to rotate in either direction, but you need to keep rotating in that direction. Facing-side Color A can be either Color B or Color C on the opposite side; facing-side Color B can be either Color A or Color C on the opposite side; and facing-side Color C can be either Color B or Color A on the opposite side. However, each color must be used in two and only two of the three types of pairs.

Here is an illustration of a three-color chart.

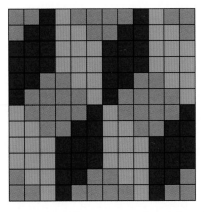

Note that if we rotate the colors in one direction …

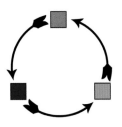

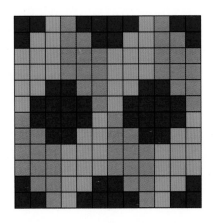

… we get one possible outcome for the opposite side.

Whereas if we rotate the colors in the other directions … We get another possible outcome.

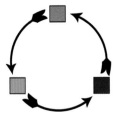

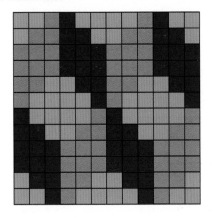

You can have Color A/Color B; Color B/Color C; Color C/Color A, or you can have Color A/Color C; Color C/Color B; Color B/Color A. It doesn't matter which way you do it, as long as you stay consistent.

END MANAGEMENT IN MULTI-COLOR DOUBLE-KNITTING

You will probably have noticed that in two-color double-knitting, your ends tend to twist around each other, necessitating some periodic pauses to untwist them in one way or another. With a third color, there is the further danger of braiding. If you consider the three ends positioned in a triangle, It is certainly possible to make a color change — usually between pairs, as opposed to between the two stitches in a pair — that pulls the point of the triangle out between the two other points. You want to avoid this as best you can.

I find the best way is to imagine that there is some solid core in the middle of the triangle. Your ends should be positioned so that they can be rotated around this imaginary core, presenting a face of the triangle with the facing-side color in front, the opposite-side color in back, and the unused color below them. If you keep rotating the triangle in this way, the worst that will happen is that the three ends will twist around each other, which is easy to undo simply by holding them up and letting your knitting dangle below.

If you manage to get into a braided situation (and in particularly bad ones, "braid" is a euphemism), you may be able to get out of it with a little trial and error while making color changes, but it is always possible to feed the source yarn balls through the holes in the mess and untangle things that way.

MULTI-COLOR TWO-PATTERN DOUBLE-KNITTING

After working out the possibilities of two-pattern work, and further working out the addition of a third color, it was a logical next step to try them together. Like two-color two-pattern double-knitting, this method uses charts that are notated literally, showing every stitch type and color rather than only one side. The addition of the third color really only presents difficulties in end management and tension; otherwise you already have all the skills you need to follow the patterns.

END MANAGEMENT IN MULTI-COLOR TWO-PATTERN DOUBLE-KNITTING

This is one area where I can't offer an easy explanation. Because the triangle rotation method doesn't work when pairs can literally have any of 9 different configurations, it is very likely that you will have to unbraid your ends more frequently than with multi-color single-pattern double-knitting. I can try to impart some wisdom, but it's a lot to keep in mind and in all likelihood you won't be able to do it 100% of the time.

You can arrange the three colors in a triangle. It doesn't matter what order they're in, but for the sake of this example, we'll say they're in the order of A-B-C. First of all, this means you'll be able to do pairs that are A/B, B/C, and C/A naturally, without any braiding, if you use the end management method from the previous section on multi-color double-knitting (page 111). Second, you can do pairs that are A/A, B/B and C/C without any trouble, as long as you keep the other two ends below while working the pair.

The problem comes when you work pairs which are A/C, C/B or B/A. In the previous end management section, I said you could use any side of the triangle with the unused end below. These three, however, represent sides of the triangle from the inside — or with the unused end on top. You should be able to create the pair by moving over the top of the unused end, which keeps your color changes from pulling ends from inside the triangle, but in reality what this does is to push the unused end through the middle of the triangle and invert the triangle direction — and begin braiding your yarn. It doesn't work much better if you leave the unused end on top and work inside the triangle. I think the best way is to do the method that inverts the triangle, mentioned above, and as soon as the pair is complete, push the unused end back into place so the braid doesn't become permanent.

...or you could just wing it, take each stitch as it comes, and do your best not to let the ends braid — and when they do, you can always untangle them in the same way as mentioned before. To be honest, that's what I do most of the time. With practice, you will find ways to unbraid as you go.

Another possibility is to actually make the triangle a physical object. I have done this to test some theories, but I haven't found a great way to actually knit a whole project with it — you'd need an extra hand. But If you want, you can cut a disc about the size of a half-dollar out of thick cardboard and punch three small holes in it, evenly spaced in a ring at about the diameter of a quarter. Cut slits from the edges down to those holes and slot your three ends into it. The holes will allow the yarn to pass through as you feed it from the source balls, and the triangle separating the ends will make it much more obvious when you do make a braid.

TENSION IN MULTI-COLOR DOUBLE-KNITTING

It is often tempting, when using a color which has not been used in a while, to pull it tight before making the stitch. Try to avoid this. Multi-color double-knitting is not terribly flexible because every pair has at least one unused strand in between its stitches. These strands can sometimes travel considerable distances, and it isn't practical to lock them into place in the middle as you would with stranded knitting. It also wouldn't serve any purpose, since you can't see them anyway, and locking strands in place doesn't keep you from pulling the strand tight when you do reach the next stitch in the strand's color. Knitting stitches are quite flexible, but yarn alone is not. Try to keep a little slack on any strand you pick up after an expanse of pairs that only use the other two colors. It will make your garment more flexible and the pattern will not distort as much when you stretch it.

PATTERN: STRUKTUR

Samples knit by Alasdair Post-Quinn, Suzanne Ress

This hat is a refinement of my first foray into three-color double-knitting, or triple-knitting for short. I stumbled across the pattern on Jessica Tromp's website (http://www.jessica-tromp.nl/) and created this pattern. I got many comments on it when Twist Collective put it atop my article on double-knitting in their Winter 2009 issue, but I didn't have a pattern at the time and didn't expect I'd be able to publish one anyway, since the chart was not originally mine. However, honesty is the best policy, and I emailed Jessica to ask if it was okay if I used this pattern in my book — and to my surprise, she agreed! The first hat I designed with it used an 8-sided decrease and spiraled up to a point — but I never liked the point, so I worked out a more complex and elegant closure, charted here.

Struktur is a German word, which Google translates to, among other things, "structure, texture, fabric, construction, weave". Considering that it also looks like a set of skeletal building blocks, I couldn't have asked for a better name for the pattern.

MATERIALS:

[Color A] Cascade 220 (100% wool); 220 yds/100g skein; #8011; 1 skein. 9 wpi.
[Color B] Cascade 220 (100% wool); 220 yds/100g skein; #9326; 1 skein. 9 wpi.
[Color C] Cascade 220 (100% wool); 220 yds/100g skein; #2448; 1 skein. 9 wpi.

1 US6/4mm circular needle, or needle size required to achieve gauge desired.
1 set US6/4mm DPNs, or needle size to match circular needle above.
Tapestry needle

GAUGE:

20sts/27 rows = 4" in double-stockinette fabric. However, because of the three-color tension, you are more likely to get 22sts/27 rows = 4" with the finished fabric. The size of the hat as written is about 20".

PATTERN NOTES AND IDEAS:

Feel free to rotate the colors in the other direction if you prefer. Just remember to be consistent and check your work.

PATTERN:

The chart is a 28-pair repeat, so sizing is done by changing needle gauge. On US6 needles, you should get a 20"

hat; on US7, you should get a 22" hat, and on US8 needles you should get a 24" hat. Swatch first to make sure, of course.

Using the standard double-knitting cast-on, with Color A as FC and Color C as TC, cast on 112 pairs or 224 total stitches, not counting the slip-knot. Remove and untie the slip-knot at the beginning, then join, being careful not to twist the cast-on edge. Before you begin, add Color B in the same orientation as the other two colors and use all three colors while working the pattern.

Each chart is worked 4 times around. Follow Chart 1a twice, then Chart 2 once, switching to DPNs when necessary. The hat should be tall enough to fold up a brim; mine is about 12" tall. If you don't want a brim, you can follow Chart 1a once instead.

Chart 1b is only included as a reference to help you make sure you're putting the correct colors on the opposite side. Check this periodically. There is no opposite-side chart for Chart 2 since by then you'll be a pro at it.

In Chart 2, the "no pair" pixels are placed oddly because, in this configuration, they show more clearly the relationship of the pattern to the decreases. I assure you, it does work if you just follow the chart. When you reach the top, cinch the remaining loops together as described in the section on Finishing (page 158).

| Color A |
| Color B |
| Color C |
| No Pair |
\\	Left-slanting Decrease
/	Right-slanting Decrease
人	Ridged Double-Decrease

CHART 1a

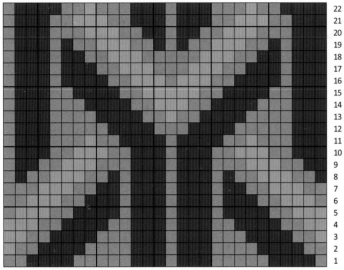

28 27 26 25 24 23 22 21 20 19 18 17 16 15 14 13 12 11 10 9 8 7 6 5 4 3 2 1

CHART 1b

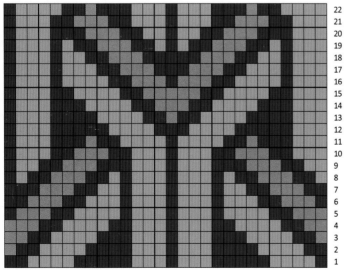

28 27 26 25 24 23 22 21 20 19 18 17 16 15 14 13 12 11 10 9 8 7 6 5 4 3 2 1

CHART 2

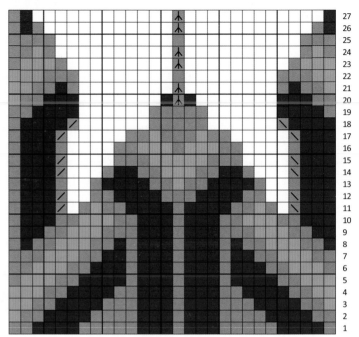

28 27 26 25 24 23 22 21 20 19 18 17 16 15 14 13 12 11 10 9 8 7 6 5 4 3 2 1

116

PATTERN: FALLING BLOCKS

Samples knit by Radka Chamberlain, Alasdair Post-Quinn

I consider this hat sort of my flagship piece. I even named it after myself (online, my handle is "fallingblox"). Despite appearances, the name "fallingblox" is not derived from this pattern — it is a reference to my erstwhile and sometime obsession with Tetris, or falling blocks games in general. I took the handle a long time before I started knitting. Also, the correct name for the facing pattern on this piece is "tumbling blocks". But the accomplishment of a two-pattern piece with three colors in every round is still something I consider worthy of a particular place of honor in my repertoire of patterns.

That said, this hat is really warm. Warm enough for a winter in the Arctic, probably. At the brim fold, it's about 5 layers thick, and it's made of alpaca-blend wool. The facing side is a typical tumbling blocks pattern; the opposite side appears to be a simple Celtic knot but is actually a chart I got from the Armenian Museum near my wife's home in Watertown, MA. The curator of the museum put together a pair of folders of charted Armenian patterns for needlework and carpets, and I am happy to use one to give a nod to my wife's heritage in this hat.

MATERIALS:

[Color A] Berroco Ultra Alpaca (50% Super Fine Alpaca/50% Peruvian Wool); 215 yds/100g skein; #6293: Spiceberry Mix; 2 skeins. 9 wpi.
[Color B] Berroco Ultra Alpaca (50% Super Fine Alpaca/50% Peruvian Wool); 215 yds/100g skein; #6227: Henna; 2 skeins. 9 wpi
[Color C] Berroco Ultra Alpaca (50% Super Fine Alpaca/50% Peruvian Wool); 215 yds/100g skein; #6244: Fig; 2 skeins. 9 wpi

1 US6/4mm 16-inch circular needle, or needle size required to achieve gauge.
1 set US6/4mm DPNs, or needle size required to match circular needle.
Tapestry needle

GAUGE:

20 sts/28 rows = 4" in double-stockinette fabric. However, because of the three-color tension, you are more likely to get 22sts/28 rows = 4" with the finished fabric. This hat benefits greatly from twisted stitches — it goes down to 6 sts/in

PATTERN NOTES AND IDEAS

Chart 1 repeated twice across in flat double-knitting makes a great scarf pattern — but you will have to remember to follow the directions for two-pattern flat double-knitting.

PATTERN:

Using the standard double-knitting cast-on, with Color A as FC and Color C as TC, cast on a multiple of 20 pairs or a multiple of 40 total stitches. When I originally designed this hat, I used 140 pairs or 7 repeats of the pattern, and it came out between 23" and 24". If you're not going to twist your stitches, you may be better off casting on 120 pairs. Don't count the slip-knot — remove and untie it before you begin the first round. Join, being careful not to twist the cast-on edge. Before you begin, add Color B in the same orientation as the other two colors and use all three colors while working the pattern.

Both charts are two-pattern charts; refer to the section on two-pattern double-knitting. Work Chart 1 twice and Chart 2 once. If you don't want a fold-up brim, you can follow Chart 1 once instead of twice. If you do this, you can return 3 of those skeins of yarn — or do another hat afterward!

When you reach the top, you should have 4 pairs for every pattern repeat. Because I started with 140 pairs, I ended up with 28 pairs left on my needles. Even if you started with 120 and now have 24, this is a lot to cinch, but cinch it anyway using the instructions in the Finishing section (page 158). Just be careful not to leave too much of a hole when it's done. Weave in all remaining ends.

CHART PREVIEWS

These are thumbnails of the facing side and opposite side of this hat. The charts on the following two pages are confusing to look at, so I find it is helpful to know what the two sides of your work are supposed to look like. The next two thumbnails are the un-interlaced forms from Chart 1; the bottom two are from Chart 2.

In the next two thumbnails, you can see the way the decreases are formed and how the cubes are reassembled around them. The reason the decreases are placed where they are is that each successive round of cubes is smaller than the one before it. The easiest way to deal with this and keep the decreases well hidden was to make the top of each cube two pixels smaller than the bottom. This means there are four decreases per pattern repeat per decrease round. This adds up to a whole lot of decreases in each decrease round, but because there are so many rounds between them, the closure ends up relatively dome-shaped, as it should.

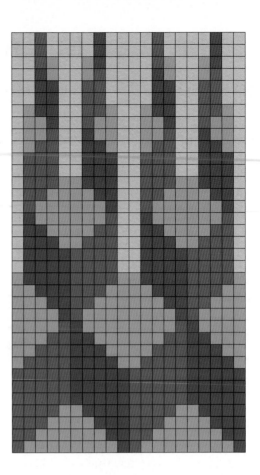

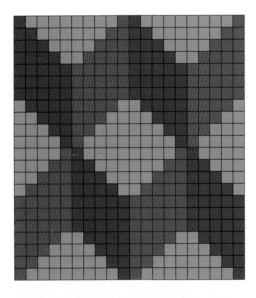

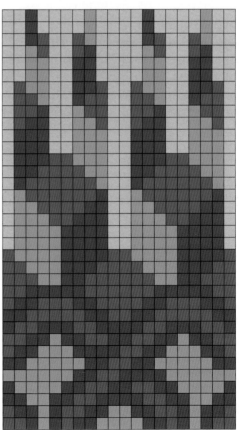

	Color A
	Color B
	Color C
	No Pair
	(Two-pattern notation) Wyib, knit with color indicated
●	(Two-pattern notation) Wyif, purl with color indicated
	(Two-pattern notation) Left-slanting Decrease with colors indicated
	(Two-pattern notation) Right-slanting Decrease with colors indicated

CHART 1

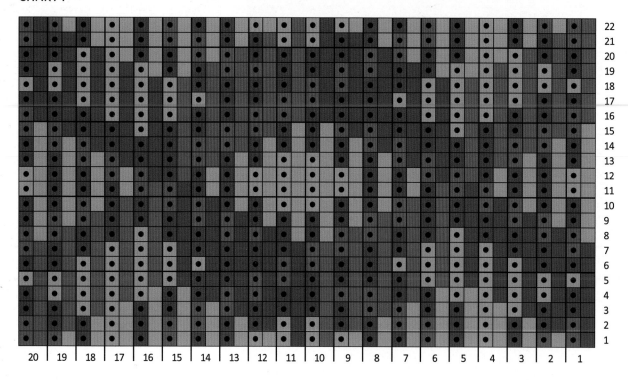

CHART 2

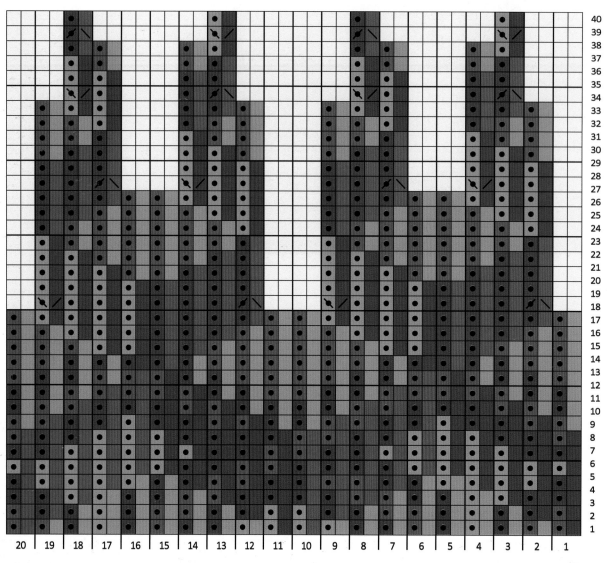

CHAPTER 6: NEW DIMENSIONS IN DOUBLE-KNITTING

Up until now, we've done some interesting things with charts and patterns, but we're still working within the constraints of double-stockinette fabric. Everything you've done so far essentially looks like stockinette on both sides, even if the colorwork goes in some unexpected directions.

You may be thinking at this point, "Oh, he's going to talk about textured double-knitting, putting ribbing and seed stitch on the fabric instead of stockinette." But I'm not terribly interested in going in that direction. I've investigated the concept to see if it's possible, and it certainly is — but you'll find that stuff in the Appendix. We're going to play with more exciting things instead.

DOUBLE-KNIT CABLES

This technique came to me while pondering reversible cables. I have knitted and designed a number of things with cables in them, and some time ago I did a Moebius scarf with a pair of thick reversible cables running all the way around it. These cables were of the 1x1 ribbing type — where the cable twist locks the 1x1 rib in a compressed state, and makes the cable look the same on both sides.

As I mentioned back in the beginning of the book, double-knitting is essentially 1x1 ribbing done in two colors — the movement of the ends should remind you of that every time you double-knit. So the jump from reversible cables to double-knit cables was not difficult.

Most people assume that cables in double-knitting are not possible or practical because the two layers are worked together. Separating the layers, doing a cable twist on both sides, then returning the pairs to a single needle again every time you want to make a cable is indeed impractical — which isn't to say it's not possible. I just think it deviates too far from double-knitting to be called such. It's not an elegant solution.

Unfortunately, the elegant solution I came up with has its limitations. Only cables that don't make use of negative space can be done in double-knitting, assuming the double-stockinette texture remains intact. There may be ways to do double-knit cables with traveling sections if you use reverse-stockinette on portions of the outer faces, but I have not experimented with this yet.

Essentially, in much the same way you do reversible cables in 1x1 ribbing, you treat the whole fabric as a single layer. Therefore, a 3x3 cable is actually 6 pairs wide, or 6x6 stitches. The resulting cables are thicker than normal because of the extra layer of fabric in between — at the location of the twist itself, there are 4 layers of fabric. As you can imagine, this makes for a very warm garment.

C2B (CABLE 2 BACK)

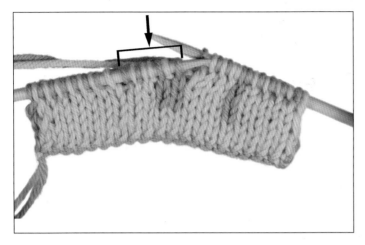

1) The next 4 pairs, shown in the bracket, will be cabled. The rightmost (color-changed) section will cross in back of the leftmost section.

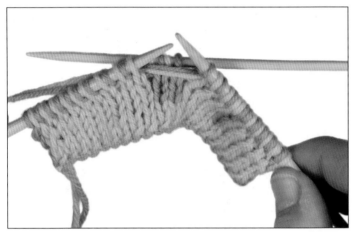

2) With ends in front, put the first two pairs on a cable needle. Move both ends to the back.

3) Matching colors, work the next knit stitch as normal…

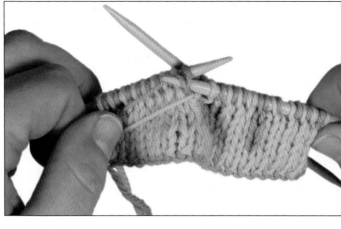

4) …and then, moving the ends to the front, work the next purl stitch as normal. Repeat for the next pair …

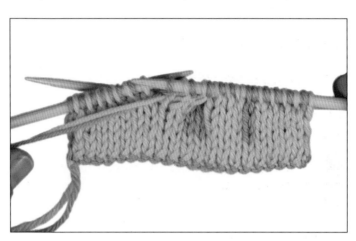

5) … like so.

6) With ends in front, pass the 2 pairs on the cable needle back onto the left needle …

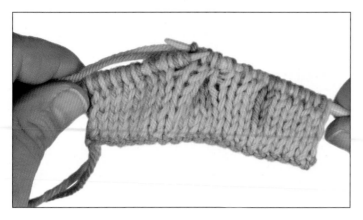

7) ... like so. Now bring the ends to the back and work the two pairs, matching colors.

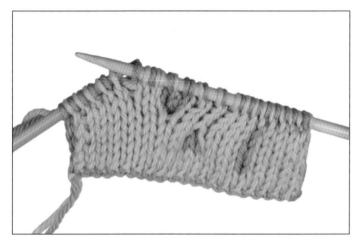

8) Here is the cable from the facing side, after working a couple more rows.

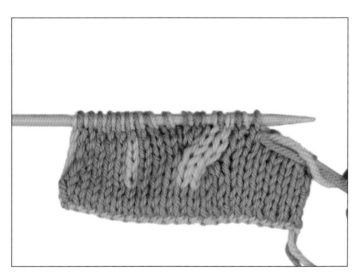

9) And here's the cable from the opposite side.

C2F (CABLE 2 FORWARD)

This cable is no different from the one illustrated above, except that the cable needle is held to the front instead of the back. A shortened version of the instructions is easier to hold in your mind anyway:

1) With ends in back, slip 2 pairs onto cable needle, hold to front.

2) Work 2 pairs in colors indicated by pattern

3) Work 2 pairs from cable needle in colors indicated by pattern.

Of course, these are only examples — the same technique works for cables of different sizes — even asymmetric cables — as dictated by the chart elements and descriptions in the key.

DOUBLE-KNIT CABLE DECREASES

While working out decreases for the crown of Vasily (page 129), I found I needed to decrease more quickly in order to keep the crown from getting pointy. At a certain point, I began to do cables In every round rather than having matching rounds between cabling rounds. This meant that I would have to work a decrease into a cable technique. The best way I could figure out was to integrate a left-slanting decrease into a C1F, making what I call a "C1FDec". It is worked like this:

Set up the C1F twist as described above. Work the first pair (previously the second pair), then before you work the second pair, re-order its stitches along with the next pair on the left needle and work a left-slanting decrease.

PATTERN: VASILY

Sample knit by Shelley Winiger

Vasily is the Russian name for St. Basil, the Catholic saint whose name unofficially graces the colorful Cathedral of the Intercession of the Virgin on the Moat in Moscow. While working on this piece, it reminded me of the patterns on the turrets of St. Basil's cathedral, so I thought it only fitting I name the piece after him.

This piece is time-consuming but all-in-all not terribly difficult. The double-knitting itself does not have much color-changing, and the reversible cables are just that. If you can do basic double-knitting and cabling, this hat won't pose too much difficulty — in theory.

If you work on this in public, expect other knitters to think it's actually entrelac, then expect heads to explode when you show them what it really is!

MATERIALS:

[Color A] Rowan Felted Tweed DK (50% merino wool, 25% alpaca, 25% viscose); 191 yds/50g skein; #151: Bilberry; 1 skein. 11 wpi.

[Color B] Rowan Felted Tweed DK (50% merino wool, 25% alpaca, 25% viscose); 191 yds/50g skein; #160: Gilt; 1 skein. 11 wpi.

[Color C] Rowan Felted Tweed DK (50% merino wool, 25% alpaca, 25% viscose); 191 yds/50g skein; #146: Herb; 1 skein. 11 wpi.

1 US4/3.5mm 16" circular needle, or size required to achieve gauge desired.
1 set US4/3.5mm DPNs, or size required to match circular above.
Tapestry needle

GAUGE:

24 sts/32 rows = 4" in double-stockinette fabric. However, because of the cables, expect about 36 sts/24 rows = 4".

PATTERN:

Cast on a multiple of 18 pairs or 36 stitches using any 2 of the 3 colors (in either configuration) in the standard double-knit cast-on. Each 18-pair segment is approximately 2" wide. For a 20(22, 24)-inch hat, cast on 180(198, 216) pairs or 360(390, 432) total stitches.

Remove the slip-knot. Add the end of the third color, join the two ends of the work, being careful not to twist the cast-on edge, and work Chart 1, following this rotation: Facing-side Color A is Color B on the opposite side; facing side Color B is Color C on the opposite side; facing side Color C is Color A on the opposite side. This is the setup row — from now on all colors worked will match the row below, and all apparent color changing will occur because of the cables.

Repeat Chart 2 around the next 36 rounds (repeat 2 times — you can repeat 3 times if you want a brim to fold up).

Follow Chart 3 to begin the decreases. This will bring your 3x3x3 braided cables down to 1x1x1.

Follow Chart 4 to complete the decreases. Using this chart, one braid will swallow another, and eventually reduce down to 1 pair for each 18-pair segment originally cast on.

At this point, you should have only Color C and Color A on the needle. Break Color B with a long enough tail for weaving in. Use the remaining two colors to cinch the top closed according to the instructions in the Finishing section (page 158).

Carefully weave in all three ends from the cast-on and the crown. Because of the cables, you will not have as much open space inside, but you will find space if you are careful about it.

Block gently if necessary and wear with pride!

	Color A
	Color B
	Color C
	No Pair
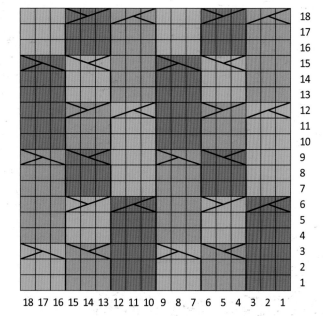	C3F (Cable 3 Forward)
	C3B (Cable 3 Back)
	C2Under3
	C2Over3
	C2F (Cable 2 Forward)
	C2B (Cable 2 Back)
	C1Under2
	C1Over2
	C1F
	C1B
	C1FDec
	Left-slanting Decrease
	Right-slanting Decrease

CHART 3

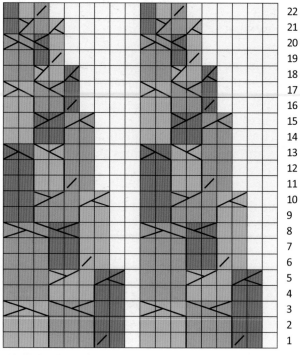

18 17 16 15 14 13 12 11 10 9 8 7 6 5 4 3 2 1

CHART 4

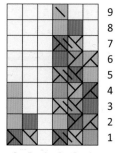

6 5 4 3 2 1

CHART 1

18 17 16 15 14 13 12 11 10 9 8 7 6 5 4 3 2 1

CHART 2

18 17 16 15 14 13 12 11 10 9 8 7 6 5 4 3 2 1

TWO-NEEDLE DOUBLE-KNITTING CAST-ON

This is a cast-on I developed for a reason other than double-knitting; I have since refined it for use in the last two patterns in this book. It is flexible in that, once the cast-on is done, there are four different directions to start the knitting — with various results. Like the standard double-knitting cast-on on page 16, I will refer to the two colors as TC and FC. This cast-on should not be done on straight needles — you must use DPNs or circular needles because both ends of the cast-on need to be accessible.

If you are already familiar with the standard double-knitting cast-on, this one will come easily. It is based on the same cast-on, with an added twist that allows the same movements to be used to cast on to two parallel needles at the same time. Because each movement generates two stitches, it is important to pay attention to the pattern, which should tell you the number of cast-on stitches on both needles, and the number of total pairs.

To begin, make a slip-knot with both colors together, and tighten the loop onto one needle. Leave a 4-6" tail for weaving in. Don't worry about which direction the slip-knot colors are facing — you will remove and untie the knot before you start working the pairs. Put the other needle on top, held loosely until the first few stitches are on it — after which time it will hold itself in place. The needle with the slip-knot on it will be called the first needle, and the other will be called the second needle. We could call them "bottom" and "top," but, since their orientation changes periodically, I decided on a less directionally-specific nomenclature.

Position your hands. With the needles in your right hand and the tails held out of the way in that hand, put your left forefinger and thumb together and put them between the two hanging active ends. The color hanging over your thumb will be called TC (thumb color) and the color hanging over your finger will be called FC (finger color).

Close the rest of your fingers over the hanging ends; spread your thumb and forefinger into a Y-shape and pull the needles back like a slingshot. The ends should come from the lower needle, pass through the middle of the Y, around each finger from the inside to the outside, and continue down into your closed hand, out the bottom of your loosely-held fist, and into your source yarn balls.

There are four ends you will need to differentiate

between. From the front to the back, you should have the outer TC, the inner TC, the inner FC and the outer FC.

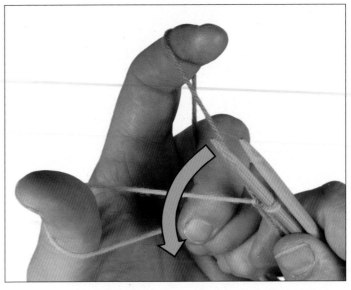

1) Start with a regular long-tail cast-on stitch. Keep the upper needle out of the way so you don't end up with a loop on it by mistake.

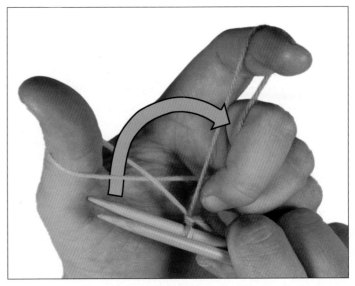

2) With your first needle in front of all the ends, bring it up underneath the outer TC. Pass the needle over the top of both inner TC and inner FC, then down between the inner and outer FC.

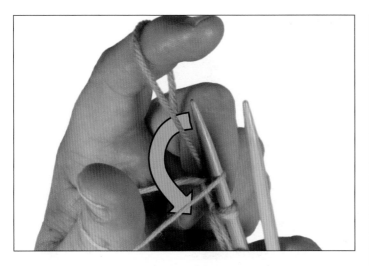

3) Pull the inner FC down with the first needle tip; with that loop of FC on your needle, pass the needle back down between the inner and outer TC ends (the same way you came in).

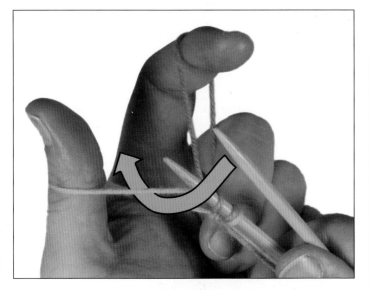

4) Now, insert the second needle into the thumb loop …

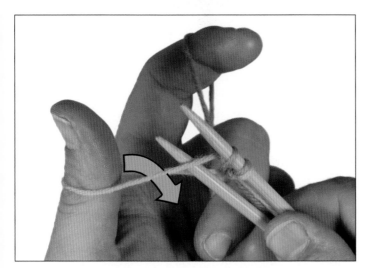

5) … drop the thumb loop, pick up the hanging end of TC on your thumb again, and tighten.

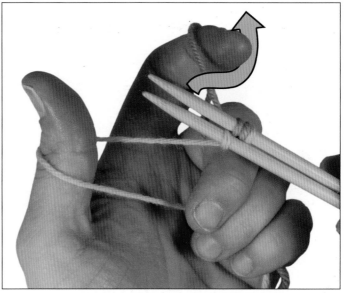

6) You should have a loop of FC on your first needle and a loop of TC on your second needle. Bring the needles in back of all the ends. Rotate them so the first needle is on the bottom again.

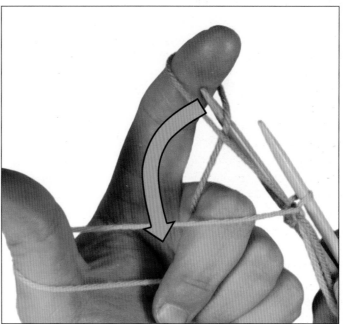

7) Bring the first needle up underneath the outer FC. Pass the needle over the top of both inner FC and TC, then down in between the inner and outer TC.

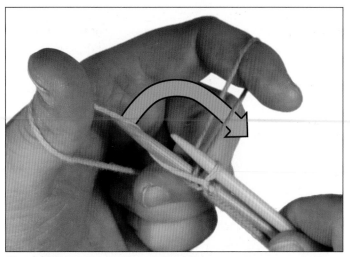

8) Pull the inner TC up with the first needle tip; with that loop of TC on your needle, pass the needle back up between the inner and outer FC ends (the same way you came in).

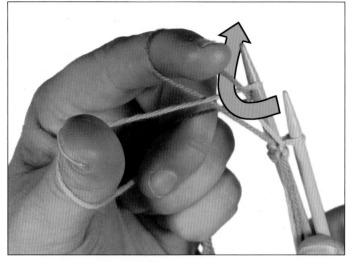

9) Now, insert the second needle into the finger loop ...

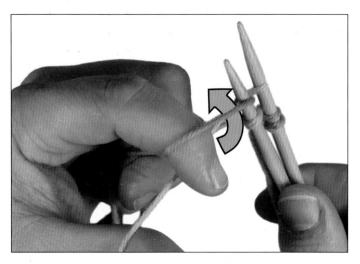

10) ... drop the finger loop, pick up the hanging end of FC on your finger again, and tighten.

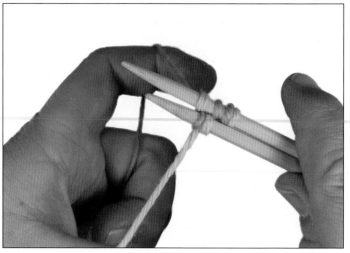

11) This has created two pairs of stitches, one on each needle. On the first needle, the first stitch is in your FC and the second in your TC. On the second needle, the colors are reversed. Continue doing one regular and one reverse long-tail cast-on stitch to continue alternating cast-on colors. I recommend you tighten this cast-on a little more than you normally would for a long-tail cast-on. It will make the first round more difficult, but the final edge will be much cleaner.

When you come to the end of the cast-on, remove the slip-knot from the far end of your lower needle and untie it before starting the first round.

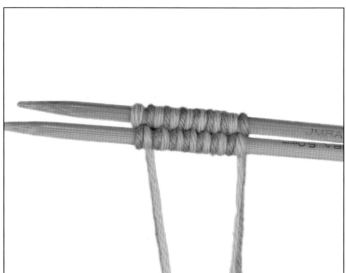

Here is a short cast-on with the slip-knot removed.

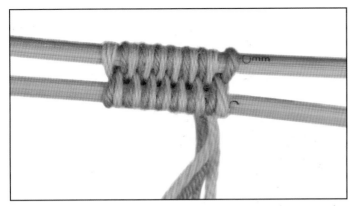

Here is the same cast-on from the concave side, spread a little bit to show the structure.

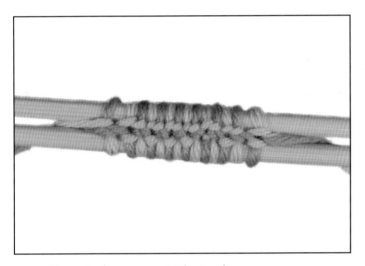

…and here is the convex (ridge) side.

LOCK-STITCHES

Lock-stitches are an interesting phenomenon I recently discovered while trying to get double-knit fabric to turn a hard right angle for shaping of my Box of Delights pattern (page 139). I have since applied them more thoroughly to other patterns and am beginning to explore the possibilities they open up.

Essentially, lock-stitches are not a double-knitting move at all. They are a single-faced knitting technique that I have adapted to work seamlessly with double-knitting. Instead of treating the pair as two separate stitches and the ends as two separate strands, you treat the pair as a single stitch and the ends as a single strand.

For a lock-knit (also called a 2K2), which is charted like this:

 ✗

knit both stitches of the next pair together using both ends held together. This literally locks the fabric together without changing the number of pairs. The resulting

two loops can either be locked again, or can be separated to continue in double-knitting. A row of lock-knit in between two rows of double-knitting will create a hard fold in the fabric — in origami terms, a valley fold, since the fabric folds toward you with a concave valley.

For a lock-purl (also called a 2P2), which is charted like this:

✗

Do the same move with a purl instead of a knit. Prepared the same way as above, this will create a mountain fold — the fabric will fold away from you with a convex ridge. The ridge (and the opposite side of the lock knit fold above) will show up as a row of purl bumps.

If the lock-knits or purls are arranged vertically rather than horizontally, the fabric will bend in the opposite direction, although the fold is not as pronounced.

While this technique can be used for shaping, it can also be used in larger expanses of knitting. For example, a flat piece done in rows of lock-knit would look like doubled garter stitch in a mingled combination of the two colors you are using. However, at any point in this garter stitch fabric, the two loops can be separated and a section of double-knitting can be created.

TRANSITIONING FROM LOCK STITCHES TO DOUBLE-KNITTING

When you make lock-stitches, you don't usually have much control over the color configuration of the resulting loops. As a matter of fact, you don't want complete control — that mingled color look is dependent on a little bit of unpredictability. However, at some point you will want to transition back to double-knitting. Technically, it's as simple as separating the pair and working each stitch separately instead of both together — this will result in double-knitting.

But if you don't discriminate when it comes to colors, the transition is going to be a little sloppy. I recommend you reorder the pairs depending on the colors you need. Each lock-stitch pair is composed of two colors in one of two possible configurations. As you come to a pair that is in the wrong configuration, pull one of the loops through the other (which one gets pulled through will depend on which is easiest to do in the specific situation, but doesn't matter) to put the loops in the correct configuration before working the pair in double-knitting.

TWO CIRCULARS AND 3 DPNS

This isn't actually exclusively a double-knitting technique, but it's necessary for the final pattern in this book, which is a seamless four-color self-lining shoulder bag with the color pattern only on the outside. It's an utterly ridiculous pattern, and one I consider a magnum opus, albeit a small one (if that's not too much of an oxymoron). It's only fitting that it requires an utterly ridiculous technique for the first quarter or so of the body.

I heard about the two-circulars method in passing, but never looked seriously at it. I never liked Magic Loop (probably partially because I can't stand metal needles, and Magic Loop seems to work best on Addi Turbos), and assumed the two-circular method would be something like that. It's not. It's much more ingenious, and I have adopted it as a preferred alternative to DPNs. I will try to impart it here, although for a better explanation, you should read Cat Bordhi's book on the topic (see the bibliography for details). The two-circulars-and-3-DPNs method is my own modification, born of necessity.

For the sake of example, take any circular knitting project — a double-knitting project would be great, perhaps even the exercise from page 30 — that you have still on the needles. You're going to need two circular needles of any length (no more than 16" is required) and 3 DPNs, all in the correct size for the piece you're working on. Divide the stitches/pairs roughly into sixths, either using markers or just writing down the number of stitches in 1/6 of your current piece. The actual fraction isn't important; you just need an oblong shape — two long sides and two short ones.

1) Starting at the current location of your active end(s), slip one circular needle into one long side (equivalent to 2/6 or 1/3 of the total stitches)

2) Slip one DPN into one short side (equivalent to 1/6)

3) Repeat 1 and 2 for the other circular and DPN.

4) You should now have the ends ready to work at the beginning of one of the long sides, currently populated by a circular needle. Pull the needle through and with the other end of the same circular needle, work across this section of your round according to your pattern.

 5) You now have the ends ready to work at the beginning of one of the short sides. Pull the circular needle in the previous section so the stitches lie only on the cord of the circular needle. This makes the section more flexible so other sections can be more easily worked. Using

the 3rd DPN, work across the DPN in the next section according to your pattern.

6) Repeat 4 and 5 for the next two sections.

You have now done a round with two circulars and 3 DPNs. The third DPN is just there to work the other two DPN sections. Repeat for as many rounds as it takes for you to get the hang of it. Then, do this:

1) Work one of the long sides with the circular needle, as before.

2) With the same circular needle, continue to work the side with the DPN in it.

3) Repeat 1 and 2 for the other 2 sides.

Your long sides are now longer, and there are no more DPNs. However, the two-circular method is now fully in play and you should be able to continue work on your project — and, if you like, finish it without use of DPNs. The two-circular method is not restricted by diameter — it's more like working two flat pieces that are connected to each other.

PATTERN: BOX OF DELIGHTS

Sample knit by Alasdair Post-Quinn

While brainstorming things to put in this book, someone suggested a little box might be just the thing for a small project, not too much of a time commitment, good for practicing a number of techniques. I thought this was a good idea, but I think I may have strayed too far from the original concept. Still, I think it can be said that this box is unique in construction — searches online for knitted boxes invariably turned up boxes with no lids, or lids knitted separately. This box not only has a lid, but a seamless construction, shaping and an integrated hinge thanks to the lock stitches used.

For practicing techniques, this is an ideal small piece — it has cast-on, bind-off, increases, decreases, color-changing and lock knits and purls. However, it's also designed to be sturdy and stand up on its own — so the fabric is tough and unyielding, for the most part. This is not something you want to hear about most knitting projects, but for a box it's not a bad thing. The bad thing is that the way I make the fabric tough is by knitting it in bulky yarn on size 4 needles. The first couple of revisions broke at least one DPN, and required plenty of resting due to stress on my hands. All this because I don't like to felt my double-knitting — I like the stitch definition. You may want to experiment with larger needles and felting — I'd love to see how it turns out.

Regarding the name, yes, this is named after the John Masefield book and my favorite bizarre BBC Christmas miniseries from childhood.

MATERIALS:

[Color A] Brown Sheep Lamb's Pride Bulky (85% wool, 15% mohair); 125 yds/113g skein; #220: Ocean Waves; 1 skein. 5-6 wpi.
[Color B] Brown Sheep Lamb's Pride Bulky (85% wool, 15% mohair); 125 yds/113g skein; #182: Regal Purple; 1 skein. 5-6 wpi.

1 set US4/3.5mm DPNs, or size needed to achieve gauge desired.
Tapestry needle

GAUGE:

18 sts/22 rows = 4" in double-stockinette fabric.

PATTERN NOTES AND IDEAS:

This pattern is best done in untwisted stitches, largely due to the difficulty of some of the increases — which will become even more difficult if worked in twisted stitches.

All increases in Chart 1: If the purl-side increase is too tight to deal with purling through the back loop, purl normally. With the density of the surrounding stitches, nobody will notice.

Chart 1, Round 5: This row's increases are tougher than normal because of the short span between them. The corresponding rows 8 and 11 are much easier.

Chart 2, Row 4: This is a wrong-side row, and the previous row doesn't help you remember that since the lock stitches will scramble the color configuration of the pairs. The lock-knits in this row are worked, of course, as lock-purls.

Chart 3 and 4: You are welcome to add more height to the box by adding more matching rounds to rounds 2-8 — or less, by subtracting rounds. You should do at least as many rounds as the height of the box lid, though.

You can also do something other than stripes if you want — the body and overhang of the box both present opportunities for small motifs, as do the large triangles comprising the top and bottom of the box.

PATTERN

Cast on 4 pairs to a single DPN, using the standard double-knitting cast-on. The configuration of the colors doesn't matter. Remove and untie the slip-knot. Divide the 4 pairs onto 4 DPNs and join, being careful not to twist. Repeat Chart 1 twice around.

Chart 2 is worked flat, across three sides of the square. The fourth side is left on the last needle – cap the needle if you feel the need. When you finish with Chart 1, turn your work. Follow Chart 2, then use the decorative bind-off.

You now have a lid. The base of the box is worked off the stitches held on the other needle. Hold the lid upside down (so the brim faces upward) and pointing away from you. 2K2 across the needle. Then, add another needle and cast on 14 pairs in either color configuration using the standard double-knitting cast-on. Repeat this with the other 2 needles (keeping a color configuration consistent with the first needle) until you have 4 DPNs and 56 total pairs, evenly distributed. Join the ends of the work, being careful not to twist the cast-on edge.

Repeat Chart 3 four times around (once on each needle). When you reach Round 10, work the first 6 pairs as indicated, then reorder the pairs on your DPNs to resemble Chart 3a. This will make the double-decreases easier. Keep in mind that the beginning of the round has not changed its location, and that the last pair worked will be a double-decrease.

When you have 8 pairs left on the needle, cinch the remaining stitches using the instructions in the Finishing section (page 158) and weave in all ends.

 Color A

Color B

No Pair

V Right-side Increase

N Left-side Increase

ᛣ Ridged Double-Decrease

ᗕ 2P2 (Lock Purl)

ᗑ 2K2 (Lock Knit)

CHART 3

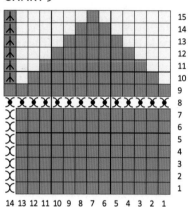

CHART 3a

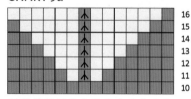

CHART 4

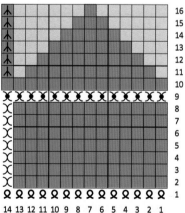

CHART 1

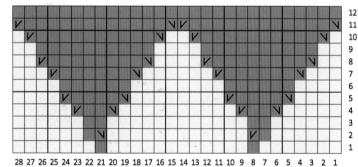

CHART 2

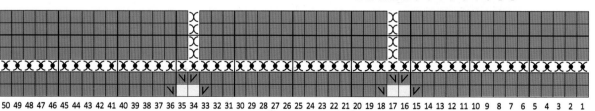

PATTERN: FOOTSIES

Samples knit by Alasdair Post-Quinn

These are the first in a series of works I plan to design integrating doubled garter stitch and double-knitting. The flexibility of this combination of techniques adds a whole new dimension to the practical application of double-knitting. This particular pattern is sized for a 1-6 month old baby. Unfortunately, sizing it up would require a whole new chart for the footprints on the bottom of the booties, so I will leave the re-sizing as an exercise to the reader until I have occasion to work on it myself. In the meantime, sizing up or down can be done by changing needle sizes or yarn weights.

This pattern includes an optional bonus two-pattern section for the top front of the booties — the R and L correspond to the right and left footprints on the bottom of the booties; however, when the booties are turned inside out, the footprints change from left to right and vice versa, so the R and the L also change places using two-pattern charts.

MATERIALS:

Purple colorway:

[Color A] Dale of Norway Baby Ull (100% wool, Superwash treated); 180 yds/50g skein; #0010: White; 1 skein. 14 wpi.
[Color B] Dale of Norway Baby Ull (100% wool, Superwash treated); 180 yds/50g skein; #5135: Purple; 1 skein. 14 wpi.

Blue colorway:

[Color A] Dale of Norway Baby Ull (100% wool, Superwash treated); 180 yds/50g skein; #5703: Light Blue; 1 skein. 14 wpi.
[Color B] Dale of Norway Baby Ull (100% wool, Superwash treated); 180 yds/50g skein; #5545: Dark Blue; 1 skein. 14 wpi.

1 set US2/2.75mm DPNs, or size required to achieve gauge desired.
Tapestry needle

GAUGE:

28 sts/40 rows = 4" in double-stockinette fabric, and 24 sts/44 rows = 4" in doubled garter stitch.

SPECIALTY STITCHES:

2K2Tog: Insert needle knitwise through next 4 stitches (2 pairs), knit with both ends together.
2P2Tog: Insert needle purlwise through next 4 stitches (2 pairs), purl with both ends together.
2P3Tog: Insert needle purlwise through next 6 stitches (3 pairs), purl with both ends together.

PATTERN

Using 2 DPNs and the 2-needle double-knitting cast-on, with Color A as FC and Color B as TC, cast on 13 pairs per needle (or 26 total pairs, 52 total stitches). You can also do this with 2 circulars, which will make the first 24 rounds much easier. However, the rest of the pattern will be written assuming you are using DPNs.

Start with the cast-on ridge on the bottom and the active ends on the right. You will be working on the back needle throughout the first section.

TOE AND BODY

Round 1: 2K2 the first pair on the first needle. Follow Chart 1, row 1 until the next-to-last pair. 2P2 the last pair and turn. 2P2 all 13 pairs across the second needle and turn.

Round 2: 2P2 the first pair on the first needle. Follow Chart 1, row 2 until the next-to-last pair on the needle. 2K2 the last pair and turn.

You should now have 15 pairs on the first needle and 13 pairs on the second. 2K2 all 13 pairs across the second needle and turn.

Round 3: 2K2 the first pair on the first needle. Follow Chart 1, row 3 until the next-to-last pair on the needle. 2P2 the last pair, then pass that pair back onto the first needle, turn. 2P2 all 13 pairs across the second needle and turn. 2P2 the first pair on the first needle, then slip it onto the front needle with the other 2P2 stitches.

You should now have 15 pairs of DK on the first needle and 15 pairs of doubled garter stitch on the second.

Rounds 4-24: Continue working Chart 1 on the DK portion and alternating rows of 2K2 and 2P2 on the remaining pairs. The sole of the bootie should be in double-knit and the top of the bootie should be in doubled garter stitch. The last half-round you do should be in 2K2. If it's not, check your work against the chart and make sure you didn't leave a row out or add an extra one in.

HEEL PREPARATION

At this point we go from rounds to rows, since we are starting the heel flap. We will return to rounds once the flap is done and the heel has been turned.

Row 25: Work row 25 of Chart 1, then turn and 2P2 the next 3 pairs on the second needle. Pass these back onto the first needle, turn.

Row 26: 2P2 the first 3 pairs, Work row 26 of Chart 1, keeping in mind that you are now working the opposite side of the chart meaning that colors and orientation are reversed. Turn, 2K2 the first 3 pairs on the second needle, then pass these back onto the first needle. You should now have 9 pairs on the doubled-garter stitch section and 21 pairs on the DK section, including the 6 border pairs. Turn. Leave the 9 pairs on their needle; cap the ends of the DPN if necessary while working on the heel.

Row 27: 2K2 the first 3 pairs, work row 27 of chart 1, 2P2 the last 3 pairs, turn.

Row 28: 2P2 the first 3 pairs, work row 28 of chart 1, 2K2 the last 3 pairs, turn.

Rows 29-34: repeat instructions for rows 27 and 28 to complete the chart. At the end of

Row 34, you should have 17 pairs on the needle.

Row 35: 2K2 first pair. 2K2Tog next two pairs. 2K2 11 pairs, 2P2Tog next two pairs, 2P2 last pair. You should have 15 pairs on the needle. Turn.

Row 36: 2P2 first pair. 2K2Tog next 2 pairs. 2K2 9 pairs,

2K2Tog next 2 pairs, 2K2 last pair. You should now have 13 pairs on the needle.

Take a fresh DPN. Slip the last pair worked onto it, then, holding both ends together, pick up and knit 6 pairs from the edge between the two needles. 2K2 all 9 pairs across the next needle. With a fourth DPN, pick up and knit 6 more pairs from the next edge, completing the circle. 2K2 1 pair from the first needle and pass that pair back to the fourth needle. You should have 11 pairs on the first needle, 7 pairs on the second, 9 pairs on the third and 7 pairs on the fourth.

CUFF

Row 37: 2P2 4 pairs. 2p3tog. 2P2 4 pairs. Wrap and turn. You should now have 9 pairs on the first needle.

Row 38: 2P2 3 pairs. 2p3tog. 2P2 3 pairs. Wrap and turn. You should now have 7 pairs on the first needle, and 30 pairs total on all needles.

Round 39: 2P2 around all needles.

Round 40: 2K2 around all needles.

Round 41-48: Repeat rounds 39-40 four more times.

Bind off loosely in 2P2. If you like, weave a ribbon into the round directly below the bound-off edge to allow you to tighten the booties. Keep in mind these are meant to be reversible, which means that putting the ribbon any lower means it may not be able to be found when the booties are reversed.

ALTERNATE CUFF WITH TWO-PATTERN DK SECTION

Row 36: 2P2 first pair. 2K2Tog next 2 pairs. 2K2 9 pairs, 2K2Tog next 2 pairs. 2K2 last pair. You should now have 13 pairs on the needle.

Take a fresh DPN. Slip the last pair worked onto it, then, holding both ends together, pick up and knit 6 pairs from the edge between the two needles. 2K2 1 pair. Work the next 7 pairs in double-knitting according to Chart 3 (if you worked Chart 1) or 4 (if you worked Chart 2). 2K2 1 pair. With a fourth DPN, pick up and knit 6 more pairs from the next edge, completing the circle. 2K2 1 pair from the first needle and pass that pair back to the fourth needle. You should have 11 pairs on the first needle, 7 pairs on the second, 9 pairs on the third and 7 pairs on the fourth.

Row 37 & 38: Same as above

Round 39: 2P2 15 pairs, follow chart 3 row 2, 2P2 8 pairs.

Round 40: 2K2 15 pairs, follow chart 3 row 3, 2K2 8 pairs.

Round 41-46: Repeat rounds 39-40 three more times, incrementing Chart 3 appropriately.

Round 47: 2P2 15 pairs, follow chart 3 row 11, 2P2 8 pairs.

Round 48: 2K2 all the way around.

Bind off as described above.

☐	Color A
▦	Color B
╲	Left-slanting Decrease
╱	Right-slanting Decrease
V	Right-side Increase
╲	Left-side Increase
☐	(Two-pattern notation) Wyib, knit with color indicated
⊡	(Two-pattern notation) Wyif, purl with color indicated

CHARTS 1 and 2

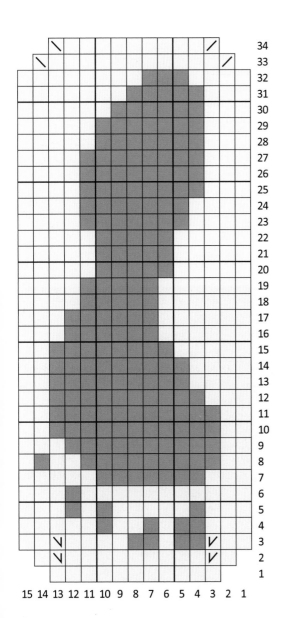

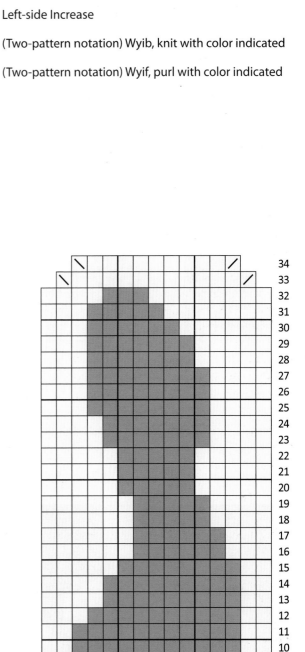

CHART 3

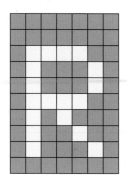 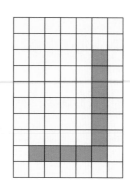

10
9
8
7
6
5
4
3
2
1

7 | 6 | 5 | 4 | 3 | 2 | 1

CHART 4

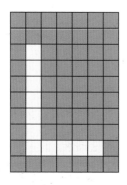 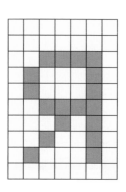

10
9
8
7
6
5
4
3
2
1

7 | 6 | 5 | 4 | 3 | 2 | 1

146

PATTERN: WHORL'D TREE

Sample knit by Alasdair Post-Quinn

I've been wanting to do something with whorl patterns on it for a while. The challenge of a 3-color whorl in a 4-direction matrix appealed to me. After some swatching, it became clear that any 4-color double-knit fabric would become both thick and inflexible. I could deal with the thickness by going down in yarn and needle sizes, but the flexibility issue was not going to be easy to solve. So I thought about items where the inflexible fabric was an asset, and settled on a bag. I toyed with various designs before deciding on the bottom-up oblong shoulder bag. This gives me a chance to use the gorgeous but inflexible decorative bind-off where people will actually see it, along the outer rim of the bag and the long edge of the flap. The bottom is naturally slightly concave and the bag likes to stand on it.

I see the design as a sort of stylized impression of a forest from inside — the brown of the roots, the green of the canopy, all tied together with the blue of the water that keeps it all alive.

MATERIALS:

Color A] Valley Yarns Northampton (100% wool); 247 yds/100g skein; #02: Natural; 3 skeins. 9 wpi.
[Color B] Valley Yarns Northampton (100% wool); 247 yds/100g skein; #33: Azure; 1 skein. 9 wpi.
[Color C] Valley Yarns Northampton (100% wool); 247 yds/100g skein; #08: Pine; 1 skein. 9 wpi.
[Color D] Valley Yarns Northampton (100% wool); 247 yds/100g skein; #28: Chestnut Heather; 1 skein. 9 wpi.

2 US6/4mm 20" circular needles, or size required to achieve gauge desired
1 set US6/4mm DPNs, or size required to match circulars above
1 set US4/3.5mm DPNs, or 2 sizes smaller than needles above
Medium to small crochet hook
2 buttons, ~1.25 inches in diameter, preferably wooden with 4 holes
1 buckle, inside width 2 inches
Small piece of iron-on facing material
Tapestry needle

GAUGE:

24 sts/32 rows = 4" in double-stockinette fabric. However, because of the four-color tension , expect about 34 sts/26 rows = 4".

PATTERN NOTES:

You may have noticed the green and brown bars to the right or left of each chart. These are guides which will help save your yarn and perhaps your sanity. When you are working a row or round that does not contain a particular color, there is no point in keeping that color. As you go, you will come across rows or rounds where there is no Color C or Color D. At the beginning of these, break the color you don't need — with enough to weave in later — and continue with three colors until the next time the color is needed, where you will re-add it. The bars on the side tell you which rows and rounds contain which colors. All rows and rounds include Colors A and B. There is one place in the strap section where both Colors C and D will be broken and then re-added later. The other benefit of this practice is that it is much simpler to untwist/untangle three colors than four — and when you remove one color from the equation temporarily, it gives you a better chance to untwist your ends.

PATTERN:

Using the two-needle double-knitting cast-on, with Color A as TC and Color B as FC, cast on 57 pairs to both needles. This will total 114 pairs (228 total stitches). Start working with the cast-on edge upward, and work on the front needle. Using the two-circular-and-3-DPNs method, begin working Chart 1a and 1b in sequence, twice around (Chart 1 is split in two pieces to make it fit on the page). In the first round, use one DPN to work the first two pairs (corresponding to pixels 13 and 14 of the pattern), then use the circular needle to complete the 55 pairs corresponding to pixels 39 to 93. Repeat for the other needle; you should have two DPNs, one at either end. The third is used when you work the pairs on the DPN in the following rounds.

Continue working Chart 1 in this way until round 18 is finished. Switch to circular needles only and continue with Chart 2. If the bottom does not lie flat, you may find it easier not to switch to circulars until partway into Chart 2. Chart 2 is repeated 6 times around the body of the bag. Follow Chart 2 once, then repeat rows 1-17 of Chart 2 until the total number of rounds done since the end of the bottom increases is 57. The bag should be approximately 11" tall from the bottom to the brim now.

Continue following row 18 in Chart 2, but stop at pixel 127. This should be 3 full repeats of row 18, plus a 22-pair partial repeat. Break off the remaining end of Color D (brown) with enough to weave in.

You should have only two ends — Colors A and B (white and blue). Using the decorative bind-off and starting with Color A, bind off the next 86 pairs. Because this bind-off is relatively inflexible, you may find the edge becomes wider than the fabric. Because the fabric is also relatively inflexible, blocking will not help here. I recommend integrating a decrease every 3rd pair, effectively reducing the number of bind-off stitches by 1/4. Because your total number of pairs is not a multiple of 4, you will have 2 extra pairs after the last decrease. Work one of them into the bind-off and leave the last pair on the needle.

Take the remaining pair and the next 19 and put them on a stitch holder. Break the two active ends with enough to weave in. Also put the 20 pairs just before the beginning of the bind-off on another stitch holder. You should now have 85 pairs on the needle.

With all 4 colors, begin to follow Chart 3a and 3b in sequence (Chart 3 is split to fit it on a page). You are now working in the flat, which means that opposite-side rows will be worked so you can't see the pattern (you are working with the plain side facing you). Pay attention to the selvedge — end each row with a pair of slips, and begin each row with a pair worked so that the facing side is Color A and the opposite side is Color B. This will give the opposite side a clean border of Color B. Pay special attention to colors C and D — make sure they are caught up in the selvedge twist so they are anchored at the edge. Follow Chart 3 until row 23.

BUTTONHOLES

Start returning on row 24 (this is an opposite-side row) but stop at pair 17. Slip pair 16 to make a selvedge, then turn and continue working the left side of the buttonhole until the end of row 29. Put these 15 pairs on a holder and break all the colors so you have room to weave in the ends.

Take all 4 colors and start again on the opposite side with Chart 3b, row 24, pixel 15. Work to Chart 3a, row 24, pixel 23; make a selvedge pair with pair 24, then continue with that expanse of pairs until the top of the buttonhole at row 29. Put these 35 pairs on another holder and break the ends. Finish up by starting with Chart 3a, row 24, pixel 23 and working as before until row 29. Break the ends and feed the held pairs back onto your needle in sequence. You should now have 61 pairs on your needle.

Start in on row 30. Row 30 is a wrong-side row but honestly, if you'd rather start on the right side, it won't matter. Work until the end of the chart and bind off, using the same 1/4 reduction as you did for the brim of the bag. To help the edge round off better, start the bind-off with an integrated decrease (SSK), and finish the bind-off with a K2tog. Since there are 49 pairs to bind off, your last two decreases will have 1 pair between them rather than 2.

Weave in the ends around the buttonholes, leaving a good length of Color B, if available, near both buttonholes. Optionally, to reinforce the buttonholes, mattress-stitch around the buttonholes with Color B, then weave in the rest.

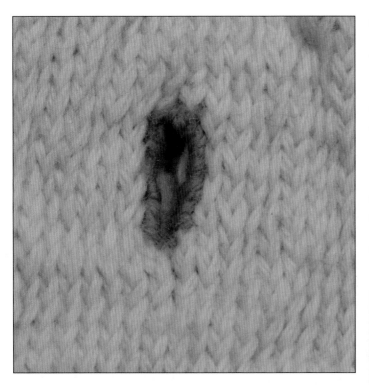

stretch a bit. Bind it off without using the decreases — it's okay if it flares a little at the end, as it will keep it from pulling through the buckle.

Put the pairs on the other holder back on the needle and follow Chart 4 once and then chart 5 once. Work two extra rows from Chart 5, breaking Color D after the first row. You should have only Colors A and B on the needle now.

Optionally, cut 1-2" of iron-on facing and iron it gently onto the back of the strap directly below the active pairs. Fold the strap around the middle of the buckle so the outside of the buckle can swivel to the outside of the strap.

Note that when a button is put in the buttonhole, it centers on one of the whorls.

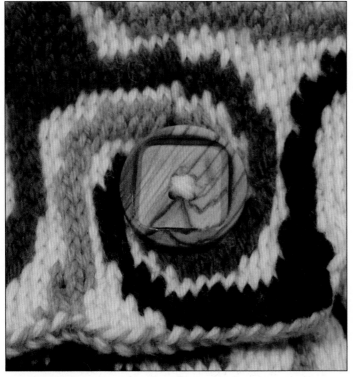

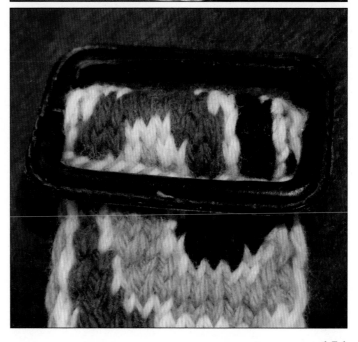

STRAPS

Put the pairs on the holder after the bind-off (on the left side of the bag) back on your needle. Follow Chart 4 once, then chart 5 8 times. The resulting strap should be 44" long. You can make it shorter if you like — it will

With a crochet hook, pull the pairs through the body of the strap, between the pairs. Because there are one fewer spaces between the pairs as there are pairs themselves, one pair will be left at the end of this move. It will be left outside the far edge, but will still be incorporated into the bind-off. You want to make a tight loop around the middle of the buckle, with as little space for the buckle to move as possible, while still keeping the fabric from distorting.

Pass the pairs you pulled through onto a US4 DPN and do the decorative bind-off by slipping the existing stitches, rather than knitting new ones — starting at the side furthest from the active ends.

Thread the long strap through the buckle and adjust to your desired length.

BUTTONS

Find two wooden buttons that have a nice tight fit through the buttonholes. The ones I used are about 1.25" in diameter. Figure out where you want them by laying the flap down against the body. Sew the buttons on with sturdy white thread, or use Color A of the yarn if you prefer. You will want to sew through both layers for security's sake — you can hide the sewn dots from view on the inside by sewing through only the front layer, but this is not secure in the long run.

Now, you have a ridiculous number of ends to weave in. Weave them in, block if necessary, and enjoy!

☐	Color A
▨	Color B
▨	Color C
▨	Color D
▨	No Pair
(	Selvedge at end of facing-side row
)	Selvedge at end of opposite-side row
V	Right-side Increase
⟍	Left-side Increase
⟍	Left-slanting Decrease
⟋	Right-slanting Decrease

CHART 1a

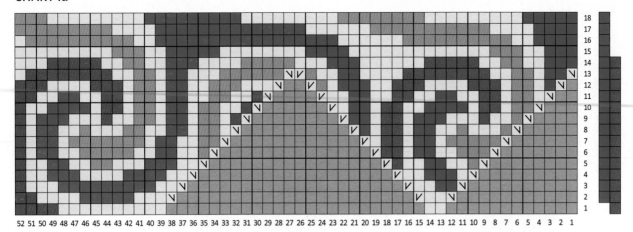

52 51 50 49 48 47 46 45 44 43 42 41 40 39 38 37 36 35 34 33 32 31 30 29 28 27 26 25 24 23 22 21 20 19 18 17 16 15 14 13 12 11 10 9 8 7 6 5 4 3 2 1

CHART 1b

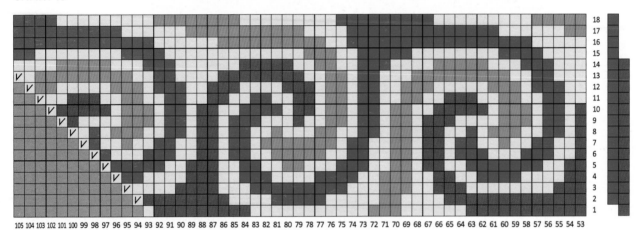

105 104 103 102 101 100 99 98 97 96 95 94 93 92 91 90 89 88 87 86 85 84 83 82 81 80 79 78 77 76 75 74 73 72 71 70 69 68 67 66 65 64 63 62 61 60 59 58 57 56 55 54 53

CHART 2

35 34 33 32 31 30 29 28 27 26 25 24 23 22 21 20 19 18 17 16 15 14 13 12 11 10 9 8 7 6 5 4 3 2 1

154

CHART 3a

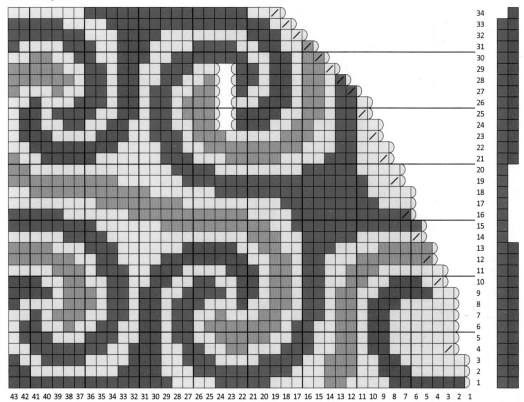

CHART 3b

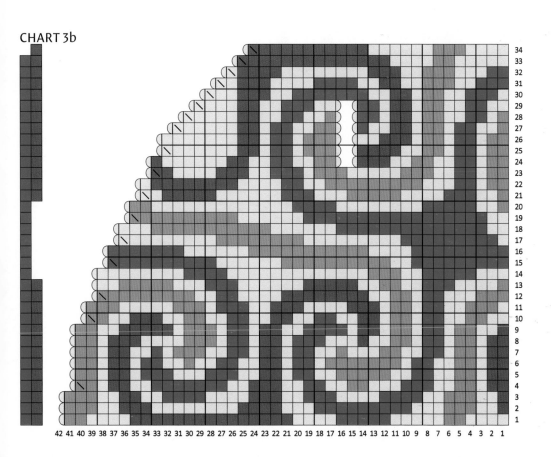

CHART 4

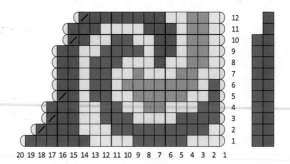

CHART 5

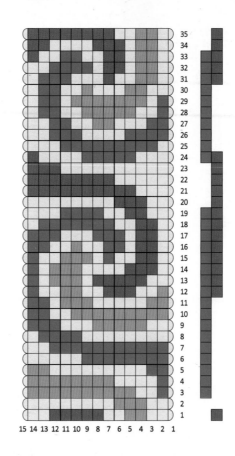

CHAPTER 7: FINISHING

I've never felt that double-knitting requires much finishing. Once your tension is correct — something that comes with practice — the finished objects often look quite attractive on their own. I've put plenty of thought into the edges and the cast-on and bind-off, but if you don't like your edges there are plenty of resources you can use to add a crocheted or other afterthought edging on. However, there are a few things unique to double-knitting that deserve some explanation.

CINCHING

When you get to the last round of a double-knit hat (for example), you'll have some relatively small number of pairs still on the needle. Whereas in single-faced knitting, you just run a tapestry needle through the stitches, in double-knitting you have two layers that must be dealt with separately.

First, if you are working in more than two colors, and you have more than two ends left at the end of the pattern, break off all colors with ample weaving-in length and choose two. In general, these are the two that correspond to the dominant color of the facing side and the dominant color of the opposite side at the closure. The unused color(s) will remain in the middle and will stick out the remaining hole in the top until woven in.

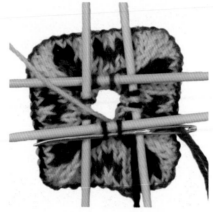

2) Thread the end of Color B onto a tapestry needle. Insert the tapestry needle into the odd-numbered loops (first, third, etc) on the outside of the first DPN and pull through, being careful not to loop the end around the DPNs. Repeat this all the way around, then once more through the knit stitches on the original DPN. Remove the tapestry needle.

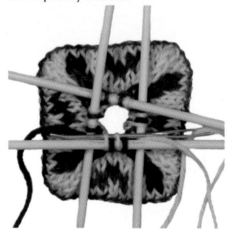

3) Thread the end of Color A onto the tapestry needle. Insert the tapestry needle into the odd-numbered loops (first, third, etc) on the inside of the first DPN and pull through, being careful not to loop the end around the DPNs. Repeat this all the way around, then once more through the purl stitches on the original DPN.

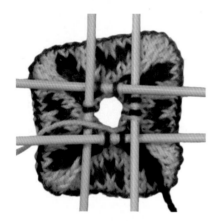

1) In the example, we have 8 pairs to be cinched. The knit stitches are predominantly Color B, so we will use Color B to cinch those. Put the end of Color A into the middle and out of the way.

4) Remove all the DPNs. Your live stitches are now secure.

5) Pass Color A (or the color you used on the inside of the DPNs) through the center hole to the other side of the work.

6) Tighten both ends. This is the facing side …

7) …and this is the opposite side.

WEAVING IN ENDS

Weaving in ends in double-knitting is one of the delights of the technique. I bet you never heard anyone say that about weaving in ends before. Normally, it's a tedious process that involves strategically running your ends through various stitches in various directions, in an attempt to ensure that it will never be seen again.

Double-knitting, however, is hollow. Nobody ever sees the inside of the work. Therefore, every piece is absolutely packed with hiding places for ends.

1) With a tapestry needle, thread one or two ends and find a likely entry point. A good entry point will be somewhere close to the exit point but not the same hole — you don't want to undo whatever stitch the ends came out of. Along the brim of a hat or other circular object, you will have a small offset between the level of the cast-on and the level of the first round. You can position the entry point to flatten the jog a little bit by inserting the tapestry needle into the gap between the first and last cast-on pairs.

2) Feed the needle through the middle of the fabric, wiggling it back and forth to make sure it stays between the layers. Check both sides to make sure you can't see the needle. I recommend you pass the needle through as many color changes as possible. Color changes are where the two fabrics change sides, and therefore they are closer together. They'll "pinch" the woven-in ends a little more at these places.

3) Poke the needle out anywhere between two stitches. If you like (and if you have enough yarn), point the needle in a different direction and pass it through the middle again.

4) When you're done, pull on the end a little bit and snip it off near the base of the exposed ends. Tug on the fabric nearby and the ends should be sucked inside.

If you're working in wool or part-wool, the layers will felt together with wear, and the ends will felt into the layers, making the weaving even more permanent.

BLOCKING

I'm not a huge fan of blocking my double-knit pieces, but I realize it's necessary sometimes. I don't have a vast amount of experience, but most blocking techniques are applicable to double-knitting as well as single-faced knitting. You can pin out your fabric to the size you want and then steam it, or whatever your preferred blocking method is. I have found one blocking technique to be very effective for one specific issue, however.

In cases where your tension is not perfect; your pairs are a little uneven or your fabric is bunching up because of the third or fourth colors running too tightly inside, you can take the piece and put it on an ironing board. Spritz it a bit with the iron or a spray bottle, then put a t-shirt or a couple of layers of similar soft natural-fiber fabric on top of it. Iron as normal, making sure not to iron directly on the double-knit fabric. You want to heat it up with a small amount of moisture and pressure; this will even out odd stitches and flatten out some of the bunching.

CHAPTER 8: READING (AND UNDERSTANDING) YOUR DOUBLE-KNITTING

THE STRUCTURE OF DOUBLE-KNIT FABRIC, IN DEPTH

We've already been over the basic structure of double-knit fabric. To sum up, there's a front and back stitch to every pair, which creates a front and back layer of fabric. Depending on the type of pattern you're looking to create, the pairs may be the same or different colors. You know that the unused strands are hidden inside the work — but how does it happen?

I've created some interesting illustrations that show you, visually, how the strands move between layers of double-knitting. I hope they'll help you better understand the structure of the fabric.

Each of these illustrations is set up in the same way:

A row or row segment is snipped out of a chart in one of the patterns in this book. To prepare the illustration, you're going to have to imagine you're looking at the top of the row, where the needles would normally be. This means you'll be looking at both layers. If the chart shows you only one layer, I've generated a second layer with reversed colors, and put it alongside the facing side layer. Because double-knit stitches are interlaced, I've put the opposite-side row chart a half-pixel off from the facing-side row chart. Then, I've separated the two rows to show how the strands move between them.

To decipher the meaning of these illustrations, you have to look at two different characteristics about the way the strands travel. You'll notice that there are two types of strand movement — lateral (one or more stitches along the same side) or crossing (from facing to opposite side or vice versa). The strands also travel short distances (between two or across three pairs) as well as long distances (four or more pairs between uses).

When a strand crosses from one side to the other, it usually signifies a color change — but more importantly to the structure of the fabric, it signifies a place where the two layers are locked together. When a strand moves laterally, the end result will be a separation between the two layers, or a hollow space. A double-knit fabric with no colors in common on either side would have no crossing strands and therefore be completely hollow. The more crossing strands, the more solid the fabric becomes — up to a point.

It is possible to do "double-knitting" all in one color, letting the opposite color travel along but never using it. This would create a fabric with crossing strands twice at every pair — theoretically a very stable fabric. However, what really occurs is 1x1 ribbing with an opposite-color strand interwoven between the knits and purls. If that other strand is twisted in at the edge, the unused end will extend across the row, and the 1x1 ribbing will be artificially held compressed. Unfortunately, it will be completely inflexible fabric because of the structure of the yarn itself.

Yarn in general doesn't change length much when pulled from end to end. Knitting is flexible because you are essentially interlinking little tightly-coiled springs. If you take a spring and compress it, then connect the two ends of the spring with something inflexible, the spring will not be able to be extended — but there will still be tension, and the spring will want to decompress, as long as there is leeway for it to do so.

However, a strand which is unused from one end of a row to the other is a very rare occurrence. It is much more common to have a strand traveling a long distance inside the work — either laterally or crossing — which is just as much of a concern when thinking about fabric flexibility.

First of all, as an example of standard double-knitting, here's a row from Silk City (page 83). This is Chart 4, Row 6. The crossing strands are occurring regularly and never extend for more than a single pair. This is because the crossings always occur between two adjacent pairs — the color changes are always mirrored on the opposite side. A fabric like this is more likely to have large hollow spaces because the only place the strands cross is at color changes.

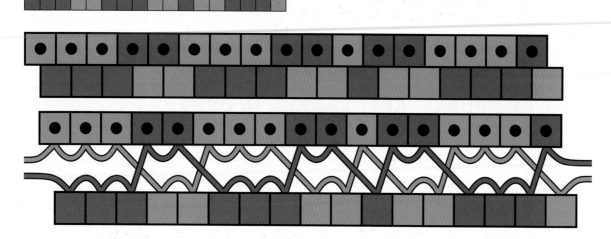

The second example is Chart 2b, Row 11 from Four Winds (page 107). You can see that the crossing occurs much more frequently and there are far fewer expanses where the two sides might separate to make hollow spaces. There are also sections where only one color is used throughout a number of pairs, and the opposite color strand must travel woven between the layers. This is the phenomenon I warned against above, but it's okay to do when the color changes on either side take up the slack, and the color changes in the prior and following rows keep the resulting ribbing from separating and the hidden strand from showing itself.

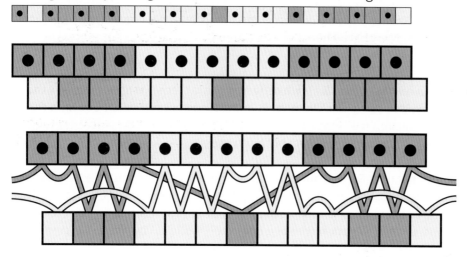

The third example is Chart 1a, Row 8 of Struktur (page 116). Here, a third color is introduced and the colors begin to rotate rather than simply reverse. Despite the fact that this is still a reversible fabric, you'll notice similarities to the structure of the fabric in the second example. Most notably, a strand may go several pairs without being used on either side and have to travel inside the work until it's used again. This makes this fabric slightly less flexible than standard reversible double-knitting, but not as inflexible as two-pattern double-knitting.

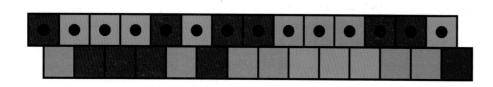

The fourth example is Chart 1, Row 10 from Falling Blocks (page 122). As we move back into the two-pattern domain with three colors, as in the fourth example, you can see that the relative inflexibility of this fabric is caused not by the crossing strands, but by the long lateral strands between color uses. This fabric is about the same in flexibility as the third example.

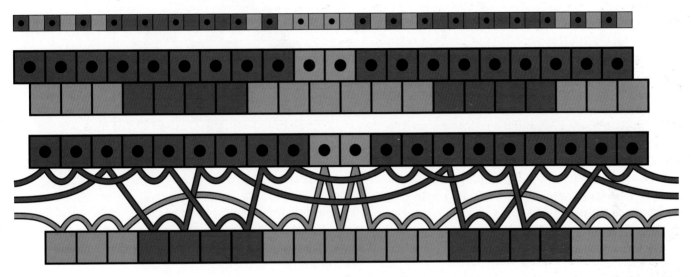

The fifth example is Chart 5, Row 15 from Whorl'd Tree. This is the strangest of the bunch. It uses the compressed 1x1 ribbing to its advantage — creating a fabric that is not only completely inflexible, but not likely to distort due to overuse of the ribbing pattern. The two sides are anchored together anytime the solid opposite-side color is used on the facing side, and anywhere else the fabric is hollow. In addition, the very long lateral strands cause the fabric to be unable to decompress — but the varying colors of those strands allow the long-unused strands to be anchored periodically and another color to take their place.

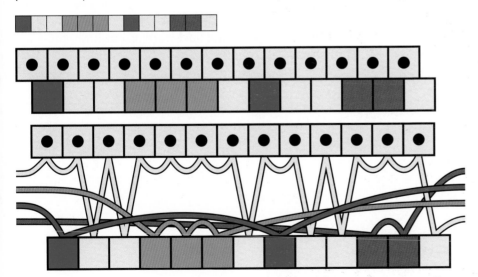

Most colorwork is done by following charts — and doubly so for double-knitting. Unfortunately, many knitters have never learned to follow charts, and have always worked from verbal instructions. While even very complex cable patterns can be communicated verbally without much trouble, I feel colorwork really requires charts. However, verbal instructions are not out of the question. I find them confusing, but you may not. In this section, I'll teach you how to read double-knitting charts, how to translate them into words, and one way I recommend for keeping more of them in your head without having to look down at your pattern as much.

First of all, I'll go over the basics of charts. The same chart may be read in two ways, depending on whether you are knitting flat or in the round. In flat knitting, odd rows are followed from right to left and even rows are followed from left to right. In circular knitting, all rounds are followed from right to left.

Take this chart, for instance, from the exercise way back in Chapter 2.

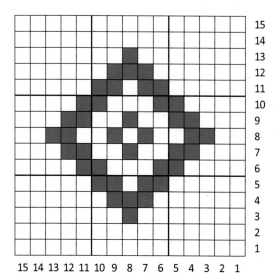

The notation used to make this chart actually assumes that every row starts from the right side and is worked from right to left, as if working in the round. However, the exercise actually has you working flat, so the row numbers are often shown on alternate sides, corresponding to facing-side (odd) and opposite-side (even) rows, like so:

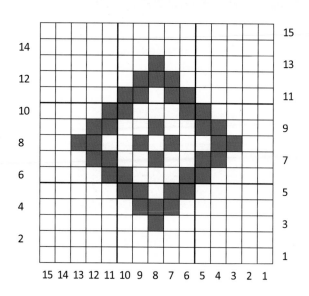

I generally don't use this sort of notation for my charts. It's a designer preference. But many people find it more intuitive since the position of the number indicates the beginning of the corresponding row.

The information above applies equally to single-faced knitting and double-knitting. However, working in flat double-knitting adds an extra ingredient to the pot. The chart you are looking at above is only one face of the work. The opposite side, reversed in color and orientation, is mentally added by the knitter. For example, let's take this orientable (in the sense that it has a specific and obvious forward and backward orientation) old-English capital Q chart.

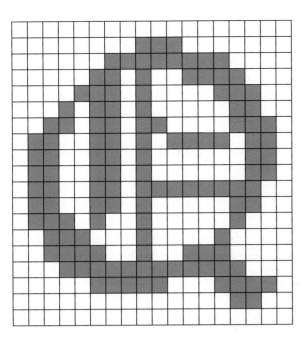

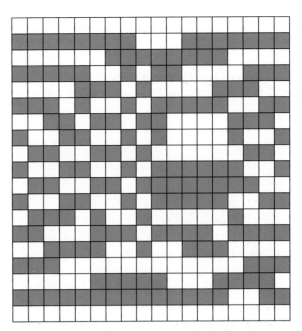

Assuming we are not correcting the opposite side to make it readable on both sides, this will be worked so that the opposite side is a mirror image of the pictured letter, in reversed colors.

This face is not illustrated; it is implied. By the rules of standard double-knitting, whenever a color is used on one side, its opposite color is used on the other side. However, when working an opposite side row — with the opposite side facing you — in flat double-knitting, in each pair you are first knitting the opposite color from the one you see on the chart, and then purling the color indicated in the chart.

In other words, to completely confuse the issue, the chart above is actually worked like this:

This is actually what you are knitting when your mind translates the opposite side every other row. Yet you wouldn't know it. Aren't brains wonderful?

DOUBLE-KNITTING VERBAL NOTATION

One way to illustrate the concepts in the previous section is to translate the chart into words.

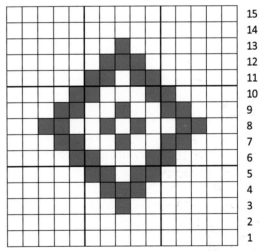

We'll return once again to this chart. Assuming Color A is the facing-side background color and Color B is the opposite-side background color, the verbal notation for it goes like this:

1) (K1A wyib, P1B wyif) to end.

2) (K1B wyib, P1A wyif) to end.

3) (K1A wyib, P1B wyif) x7, K1B wyib, P1A wyif, (K1A wyib, P1B wyif) x7

4) (K1B wyib, P1A wyif) x6, (K1A wyib, P1B wyif) x3, (K1B wyib, P1A wyif) x6

5) (K1A wyib, P1B wyif) x5, (K1B wyib, P1A wyif) x2, K1A wyib, P1B wyif, (K1B wyib, P1A wyif) x2, (K1A wyib, P1B wyif) x5

6) (K1B wyib, P1A wyif) x4, (K1A wyib, P1B wyif) x2, (K1B wyib, P1A wyif) x3, (K1A wyib, P1B wyif) x2, (K1B wyib, P1A wyif) x4

7) (K1A wyib, P1B wyif) x3, (K1B wyib, P1A wyif) x2, (K1A wyib, P1B wyif) x2, K1B wyib, P1A wyif, (K1A wyib, P1B wyif) x2, (K1B wyib, P1A wyif) x2, (K1A wyib, P1B wyif) x3

8) (K1B wyib, P1A wyif) x2, (K1A wyib, P1B wyif) x2, (K1B wyib, P1A wyif) x2, K1A wyib, P1B wyif, K1B wyib, P1A wyif, K1A wyib, P1B wyif, (K1B wyib, P1A wyif) x2, (K1A wyib, P1B wyif) x2, (K1B wyib, P1A wyif) x2

9) Same as row 7

10) Same as row 6

11) Same as row 5

12) Same as row 4

13) Same as row 3

14) Same as row 2

15) Same as row 1

As you can see, in the even-numbered rows, the first pair is worked with colors reversed from the first pair in the odd-numbered rows, even though you can see in the chart that the two pixels are the same color.

The formula for translating your own standard double-knitting charts into verbal notation goes like this:

1) Choose which color will be designated as Color A and which will be Color B. Color A is usually the background color of the facing side. If there is no clear background color, just choose one and be consistent with it.

2) For odd (facing-side) rows or if the work is in the round, replace Color A with "K1A wyib, P1B wyif" and Color B with "K1B wyib, P1A wyif". In cases where there are multiple pixels of the same color adjacent to one another, you may want to use a multiplier (e.g. "x7") to save space.

3) For even (opposite-side) rows, read the row backwards and replace Color A with "K1B wyib, P1A wyif" and Color B with "K1A wyib, P1B wyif". The statement about multipliers in step 2 above applies here too. This is only applicable to flat double-knitting, since double-knitting in the round has no opposite-side rows.

DOUBLE-KNITTING NUMERICAL NOTATION

Because I find the verbal notation cumbersome and confusing, I prefer instead to streamline the whole thing using the multipliers. If you've internalized the rules about yarn positioning, you can remove the "wyib" and "wyif" because you will already automatically do that. If you've also internalized the relationship of colors in standard double-knitting pairs and understand the reversal of colors on the opposite side, you can do away with color designations entirely and simply notate the position of color changes.

In order to do this effectively, especially for all-over patterns which may or may not always start each row with a background-colored pixel, you have to use the row below to guide you, if only to start. I use the concept of "matching" or "switched" to think about this. If a row starts with the same color configuration as the pixel below it, it is considered to be "matching"; if it starts with the opposite color configuration, it is considered to be "switched".

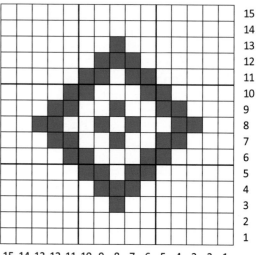

In the first row, you'll need to notate the color of the first pixel. In each following row, once you've established the color configuration (matching/switched) of the pair you'll be starting on, you count the number of pixels in that configuration, then the number of pixels in the opposite configuration, and so on. This is the same count you'd do if you were counting for the multipliers in verbal notation, above. Separate the multipliers with a comma every time there's a color change, and this is what your notation will look like:

1) (A) 15

2) (match) 15

3) (match) 7,1,7

4) (match) 6,3,6

5) (match) 5,2,1,2,5

6) (match) 4,2,3,2,4

7) (match) 3,2,2,1,2,2,3

8) (match) 2,2,2,1,1,1,2,2,2

9) (match) 3,2,2,1,2,2,3

10) (match) 4,2,3,2,4

11) (match) 5,2,1,2,5

12) (match) 6,3,6

13) (match) 7,1,7

14) (match) 15

15) (match) 15

Note that the multipliers in each row will add up to 15 in this pattern, since that is the number of cast-on pairs and there are no increases or decreases.

This is not something I ever really write down — because I am comfortable with charts — but it is what is actually going through my brain as I work from the chart. But you can write it down if it helps you. I think you'll agree that it's much more intuitive and easy to remember than the full verbal notation — and with luck, it will go a long way toward helping you to not have to write it down in the future.

Once you get beyond standard double-knitting and get into multiple colors, pixels which include other chart elements, two-pattern work, etc, you will have to develop your own mnemonic device to keep track of those pairs. But with this base of knowledge, you should be able to get there more quickly.

READING YOUR DOUBLE-KNITTING

Now that you understand how to read your charts, you'll have to figure out how to keep track of where you are in your chart. There are grid lines to help with this every 5 pixels and rows on most charts; many people use tape, or magnets, or just mark off each row as it's completed. However, if you can look at your knitting and determine where you are in your pattern, and also double-check your work for any mistakes, you'll be able to follow even the most complex of charts without any physical markers at all.

The first thing to realize while working on any knitted piece — double-knitting or single-faced knitting — is that the last row or round you completed is still on your needle. The row or round that is visible as recognizable stitches below the needle is the row before the one you just completed. So, if you're picking up your work after a hiatus, the first thing you'll need to do is to identify which row you are on. You can look at the row that's visible just below the needle, find the corresponding row in the pattern, skip a row and start working on the row two above. Make sure you're looking at your work from the facing side when you do this.

As you begin your work, especially if you are new to double-knitting, you may find yourself pausing to check your work periodically to make sure you haven't made a mistake. Fixing a mistake shortly after you made it is much easier than fixing it in the next row or round, or further on in the work (see the section on Troubleshooting, page 169).

Depending on the techniques used in your double-knitting (standard, two-pattern, multi-color, etc) this checking is done in different ways.

CHECKING YOUR WORK IN STANDARD DOUBLE-KNITTING

As you've already read, the pairs keep their structure but switch their colors when a color change is made. When a single pair in a row is color-changed, the eye is drawn to the two pairs of stitches of the same color next to each other, and it is sometimes hard to force the mind to separate those into parts of adjacent pairs. So I have a couple of simple rules that will help you get past this barrier:

1) In standard double-knitting, you should never have three or more stitches of the same color next to each other. Two is fine — the second stitch of one pair and the first stitch of the next are always the same color when a color change is made — but when three stitches of the same color are next to each other, it means you have one pair that is comprised of two stitches of the same color.

2) Turn your work so you're looking at the facing side. Starting with the first stitch on the needle, look at every other stitch and make sure it's the correct color according to the pattern. Ignore the second stitch in every pair — if rule 1 passes, you can be assured that all of the second stitches are correct.

If rule 1 does not apply, and the facing-side stitches on the needle match the chart row you've just finished according to rule 2, you're all set. If your work doesn't pass inspection using either rule, you can un-knit back to the problem pair and fix it before going on (for un-knitting help, see the section on Troubleshooting, page 169).

CHECKING YOUR WORK IN MULTI-COLOR DOUBLE-KNITTING

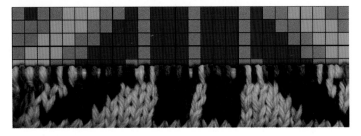

Rule 1 for standard double-knitting also applies here: no pair should have two stitches of the same color, so a segment that has three or more stitches of the same color is definitely a problem location. However, it's not as simple as that — you can't guarantee that you'll be able to identify a same-color pair simply by finding a three-stitch grouping of a single color. Since there is now at least one more color in the mix, checking multi-color

double-knitting requires a little more thought and is a little less formulaic.

1) Identify the rotation of colors, as described in the section on multi-color double-knitting on page 111. This means a pair should always be one of the possible valid configurations of the colors you are working in. Make sure you are looking at the facing side; then go across your row, making sure that all the pairs are in one of those possible configurations.

2) When you have ascertained that there are no incorrectly-rotated pairs, look at every other stitch starting with the first, and match it to the row of the pattern you're working on. Ignore the second stitch in each pair — if rule 1 has passed, the second stitch will be correct.

If rule 1 and rule 2 both pass, your row is all set. If either one fails, you can un-knit and make the correction you need.

CHECKING YOUR WORK IN TWO-PATTERN DOUBLE-KNITTING

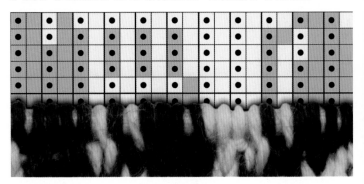

Despite the increased complexity of the technique, two-pattern double-knitting is actually much easier to double-check than standard double-knitting. This is because the charts for two-pattern work are literal: every stitch is depicted as a separate pixel in the chart. You can check your work by simply making sure the stitches on the needle match the row or round in question. This works no matter how many colors you are using.

CHAPTER 9: TROUBLESHOOTING

I like to tell my students that the best way to fix mistakes in double-knitting is not to make any.

Of course, I then proceed to tell them how to fix their mistakes. Double-knitting mistakes are, as you might expect, often doubly difficult to fix, and ripping out double-knitting is a hair-raising experience, if you plan on feeding the needle back in somewhere. But I can help keep you sane with a few tips.

These are some of the common issues you may run into in double-knitting, and how to fix them. I am not including issues that are common to both single-faced knitting and double-knitting such as tension problems — those are fixed with practice.

I HAVE DOTS BETWEEN MY STITCHES!

This is one of the most common complaints I hear from people taking my workshops. Early on in your double-knitting, you may see these little dots of the opposite-side color between your facing-side stitches. These will only happen right under the needle, and they're a complete false alarm. What you are seeing is the purl bumps from the opposite side of the work peeking out between your knits. Because double-knitted stitches are interlaced and forced to separate a little on the needle, you may see this phenomenon close to the needle, before the layers have the space to relax and spread out into their normal shape. It's not really a problem — work the next row or round and those dots will go away … but of course, you'll probably get a new crop of them too.

I HAVE BARS ON THE OUTSIDE OF MY WORK!

This happens in certain circumstances when you don't move both (or all) of the ends together between stitches. The purpose of moving them all together is so that they stay inside the work between uses. In standard double-knitting, there is never more than a strand of 2 stitches' width, but even with a single-stitch strand, it is possible to end up with a bar on the outside if you don't keep both ends together as you move between knit and purl or vice versa.

The phenomenon is easily fixed, however, as long as it is occurring only on one side of the work. If there is a bar on the outside of both stitches in a pair, there is a good chance the bars will be interlinked and you will only be able to fix one of them. In cases like that, see the section later in this chapter called "I made a mistake some stitches ago and want to go back!"

1) Work as normal up to the stitch that the bar crosses over. Put the needle under the bar, through the stitch purlwise, and back out from under the bar the same way you came in.

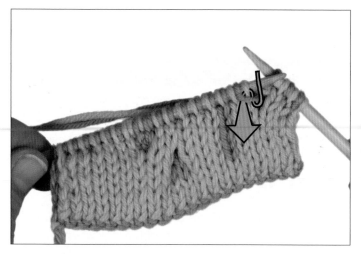

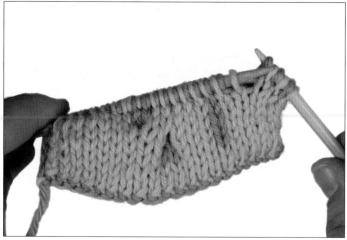

2) The stitch is now divided in half by the bar. Keeping the half that's on your right needle, slip off the half that's on your left needle.

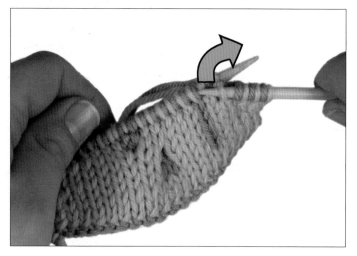

3) The bar is now inside your work rather than outside.

Pass the knit stitch on your right needle back to the left needle …

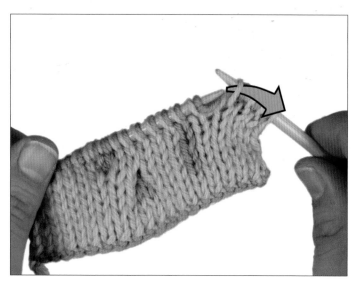

4) … and keep working as if nothing had happened!

These instructions are of course only for a bar on the facing side — the technique is the same for one on the opposite side, but you will be in opposite colors and facing away from you. You can turn the work around if that makes it easier.

I DROPPED A STITCH!

The easiest way to deal with a dropped stitch in double-knitting is the same as it is in single-faced knitting — with a crochet hook. Dropped stitches in double-knitting are not usually as much of a problem — as long as only one stitch in a pair is dropped. Since the fabric is held together on the opposite side, the completed fabric on either side of the dropped stitch does not necessarily act to pull the stitch further out of the loop below it. In fact, the most common cause of the stitch coming out of the loop below (and so on) is your attempt to get the stitch back on the needle, which can pull on the stitches below. Get some other item, such as a stitch holder or cable needle, into the stitch to stabilize it while you go dig for a crochet hook.

I'm not going to go into the details of laddering up with a crochet hook — they're the same in double-knitting as they are in single-faced knitting. The only issue is if the dropped stitch falls far enough down the ladder that it goes through a color change. This may require some finesse with the crochet hook, but it is fixable — and if you find it too frustrating, you can visit the segment of this chapter entitled "I made a mistake some stitches ago and want to go back!"

I MADE A COLOR CHANGE I SHOULDN'T HAVE (OR VICE VERSA)!

This is the problem I run into most frequently. Perhaps the color pattern is very complex; perhaps I miscounted; perhaps I was simply not paying attention. In any case, it turns out that there's a color change where there shouldn't be one, or no color change where there should be one. Most often, I notice this while working the next row or round — and I am about to make a stitch and notice that the color I am working into is not the color I expected.

As long as you completed the incorrect color pair — i.e. the purl in the pair is still the opposite color from the knit, and therefore also wrong — you will have no problem correcting the issue. The procedure is a little weird but it beats un-knitting the piece just to make a single correction.

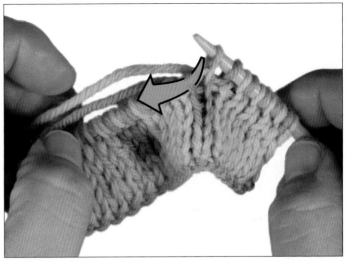

3) Put the picked up stitch on the right needle …

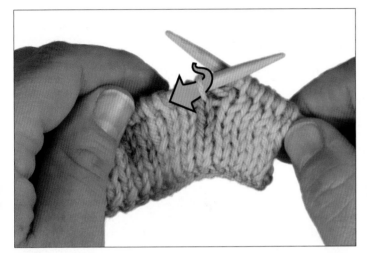

1) Work as normal — or slip stitches — up to the pair just before the one that is incorrect. The next stitch on th left needle should be the first in the pair you need to correct. Slip that first stitch onto the right needle.

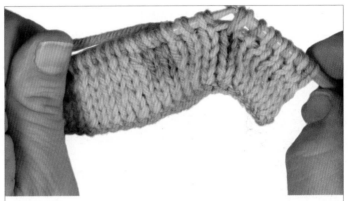

4) … like so.

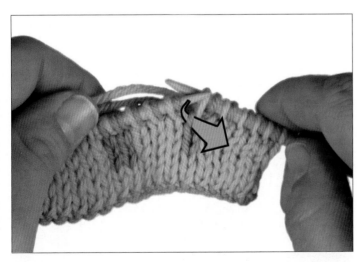

2) With both ends in back, insert the left needle into the knit stitch below the current stitch on the right needle, from back to front.

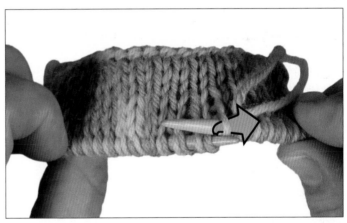

5) Flip the work up a little so you can see the back. Insert the right needle into the purl stitch below the next stitch on the left needle, from front to back, and put it on the left needle.

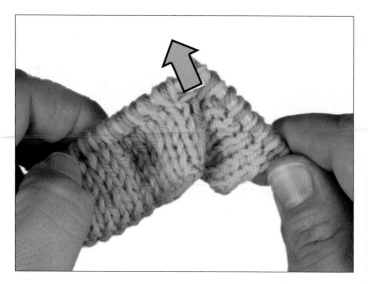

6) Using the left needle, pull the second stitch on the right needle out from under the picked-up stitch. This will create a loose loop in between the needles.

7) Using the right needle, pull the second stitch on the left needle out from under the picked-up stitch. This will create another loose loop in the opposite color.

8) Take the right needle and pass it underneath the loop that came from the right needle. Pick up the other loop

from back to front, pulling it back through the loop you went underneath. If you are making a twisted stitch, pick it up from front to back instead.

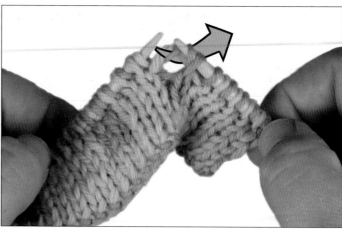

9) With the left needle, pick up the other loose loop from front to back, or back to front if working in twisted stitches.

10) Insert the left needle into the second stitch on the right needle …

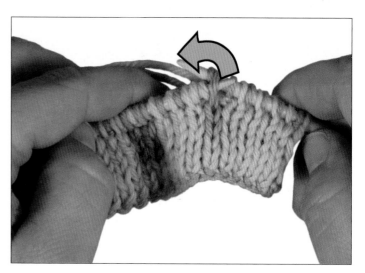

11) … and pull it over the first stitch and off the needle.

12) This is the same procedure, in progress.

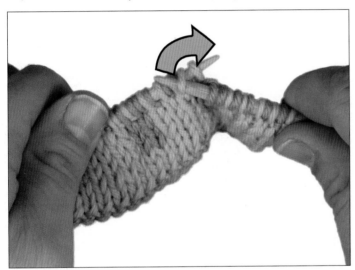

13) Insert the right needle into the second stitch on the left needle and pull it over the first stitch and off the needle.

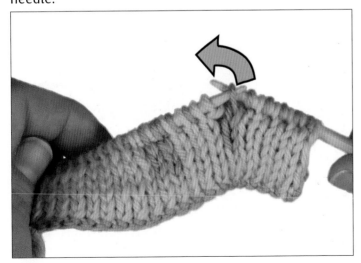

14) Pass the stitch on the right needle back onto the left needle to reassemble the pair …

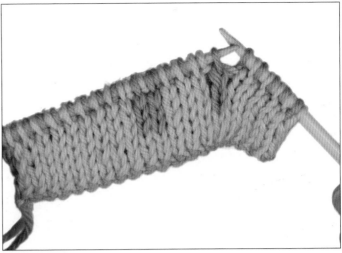

15) … and keep working as if nothing had gone wrong!

However, if you knit and purled the same color in a single pair (either by mistake or because you are doing two-pattern double-knitting), you may be out of luck. While there will be an unused strand of the other color floating inside the pair, it will likely have too much tension on it to be made into another stitch — and the same is true of the other color, but in the opposite direction — there will be another stitch worth of yarn with nowhere to go. The same issue crops up with multi-color double-knitting as well. In cases like this, it is almost always a better bet to just read on to the next section.

I MADE A MISTAKE SOME STITCHES AGO AND WANT TO GO BACK!

If all other possible solutions are exhausted, it may be time to bite the bullet and un-knit your work. I am aware of the cutesy names knitters have come up with for this section — "knit" backwards is "tink", and ripping out stitches is called "frogging". But that will be the last time you hear those terms in this book. I'm not a fan of cute words, disingenuously used to lessen the blow when you have to perform these unpleasant tasks. It doesn't change the fact that you sometimes have to undo work you've done so that you can be happy about the work when it's finished. It's a royal pain in the backside, and cute words won't change that. Swearing may be more appropriate.

You have two alternatives, depending on how far back the mistake is.

First, you can un-knit your work. This involves going back stitch by stitch until you've arrived at the point of the mistake, where it can be undone and the work can continue. The important thing to remember is that you still need to bring your ends together to the front and the back as you go, to keep the newly-freed end from getting caught inside subsequent pairs.

1) Bring both ends to the front. Because we are working backwards, the first stitch to be un-knitted will be from the opposite side.

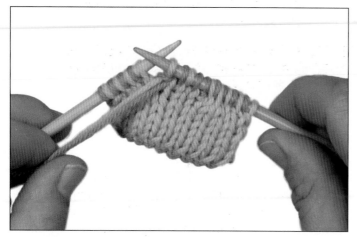

2) Flip your work up a bit so you can see the back. Insert your left needle into the stitch below the first stitch on the right needle, from front to back.

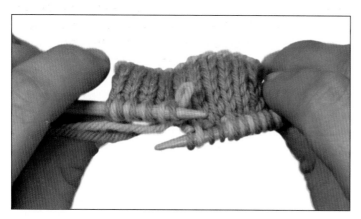

3) Slip off the first stitch on the right needle, and pull the end corresponding to its color until the loop pulls out completely.

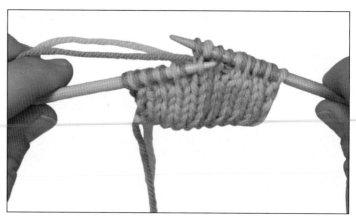

4) Bring the ends to the back, then insert your left needle into the stitch below the next stitch on the right needle, from front to back. You want to keep the left needle on the front of the work, however, so the best way to do this is to insert the needle under the furthest strand of the stitch, as shown.

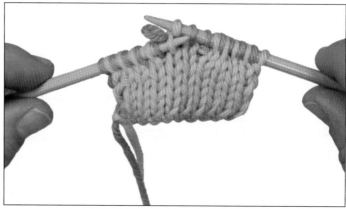

5) Slip off the first stitch on the right needle, and pull the end corresponding to its color until the loop pulls out completely.

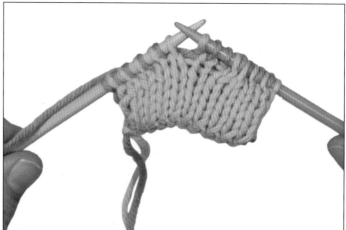

6) You have now undone one pair. Bring the ends to the front again and continue un-knitting as needed, or leave them in the back and continue forward.

Your other alternative is to rip the work out and carefully feed the needle back in below the area where the mistake was. This is best done when the mistake is a number of rows or rounds back, and un-knitting it would be prohibitively time-consuming. Depending on how tight your gauge is, you may find that the resulting loops will easily accept the needle with minimal fuss; if not, you can use a thinner needle to catch the loose loops and then slip the loops onto the correct needle once they are secure.

There are a couple of caveats here:

First, it may be hard to figure out which stitch goes where. The important thing is to take it one pair at a time, alternating knit and purl. The ends have to begin somewhere — if you start feeding in the needle on the freshly-ripped (left) side of the place where the ends are, you will know that the place you start is a valid pair. If you suspect that your pairs are off by a stitch — a knit stitch appears to have as its corresponding purl a stitch you think used to be one pair earlier or later — then you'll have to pull out the needle and start again.

Second, don't worry about the orientation of the stitch (twisted or untwisted). Your priority is to get the stitches on the needle so they don't fall further and force you to use a crochet hook. You can always correct the orientation of the stitches one by one as you go through the next row — you can even knit or purl through the back loop to twist or untwist as needed without reorienting the stitch. Once you're done with that row or round, the stitches will all be in the correct orientation and you can continue.

You can avoid some of this anguish with a lifeline. Most often used in lace, another knitting discipline that is arguably even more difficult to rip back, a lifeline is simply a length of yarn or string run through the loops with a tapestry needle at a particular place (usually when you are certain there are no mistakes below it), and tied off to keep it from falling out. This string runs in place of a needle, while being flexible enough to be unnoticeable while working on subsequent rows or rounds. If you have to rip back, you can rip back to the place the lifeline was inserted; the end being pulled out will not easily be undone since there is a string running through its loops. Lifelines in double-knitting can be tricky — it's important to make sure the line really does pass through all of the stitches. This can be difficult to ascertain since the stitches are close together and it is hard to see the half of them that are on the opposite side. It's much easier on the cord of a circular needle, since the stitches are usually larger than the cord, but at some point you will need to run your tapestry needle through stitches on the

needle itself. Once the lifeline is in, the next row will be rather annoying to work, since there will be an extra strand to navigate around. I recommend you use dental floss for the lifeline — it's usually readily available, comes in a handy container with its own cutter, and is slippery enough to pass through your stitches without catching on your yarn.

I JUST NOTICED A MISSING COLOR CHANGE WAY DOWN NEAR THE BEGINNING!

Fixing a missing or incorrect color change a long way down your work will depend on how much of a perfectionist you are. You already have my tips for ripping out your work — I feel this is a last-resort sort of thing, and shouldn't be done unless you have quite a number of problems and are confident you will be able to take care of all of them by simply re-working the fabric.

Likewise you already have my tips for laddering down — in this case, you would need to undo one entire pair and ladder the entire work down to the pair that needs fixing. Then, cross the two colors and ladder back up with a crochet hook. Again, this can be very difficult to do if you're working in two-pattern or multi-color double-knitting, so you may want to think about the last solution

Duplicate-stitching is a quick and easy way to "fix" an incorrectly placed color which is too far back to consider fixing any other way. The resulting stitch may have a little more "dimension" than its surrounding peers, but you will probably be the only one to notice that. I won't go into detail about how to duplicate-stitch — there are countless instructions in other books and online. The one thing that is different about duplicate stitching in double-knitting is that you can't see the purl side of the work to anchor the strand beforehand. This will take a little finesse as you may need to anchor the strand through the middle of and in between stitches from the front.

AFTERWORD

When I look back at the documentation I wrote for workshops I taught during the early part of my double-knitting career, I'm amused about how naïve — yet self-assured — my writing seemed. And yet, I was successful in getting people to that "A-Ha!" moment I strive for, even then. I'm sure that parts of this book will look the same way to me five years from now as well. But the important thing is that I've helped you to better understand this technique. It is my hope that this text will become a resource for generations of knitters to come, and that through my explanations, I will guide more knitters to that "A-Ha! " moment than I could possibly have reached using workshops alone.

But if someone else learns what I've taught, takes it to the next level and writes his or her own book that eclipses mine, I will be just as glad for my role in pushing double-knitting to new heights.

I hope I've been as clear as possible in all facets of this book, and that all my explanations and patterns need no further elaboration, but I'm sure I've missed something somewhere, and I'd really appreciate it if you let me know if something's unclear. I hope the initial printing of this book will be successful enough to allow me to print again — and while I'd love it if nothing needed to be changed from printing to printing, I'm not perfect and I'm sure there will be some little changes here and there.

Meanwhile, if there are any errata to post, I will do so at my blog at www.fallingblox.com. If you find a mistake, an omission, or just something you want further clarified, you are welcome to email me at doubleknitting@gmail.com. If your email triggers a change to the text, you'll be thanked in the acknowledgements page for your service to the world of double-knitting!

Please also visit the double-knitting group on Ravelry.com, or join the doubleknitting yahoo group to tap into the collective knowledge of thousands of other double-knitters like you!

APPENDIX

These are techniques not used in any of my patterns, but worth learning anyway if you're interested in how double-knitting came to be, and where else it might go.

SLIP-STITCH DOUBLE-KNITTING

Slip-stitch double-knitting is more time-consuming, less flexible when it comes to adapting single-face techniques, and harder to get a clean edge with. So why bother? This is the technique I learned first, and if we are the sum of our experiences, then I might not be writing this book had I not learned the harder way first. I believe that learning slip-stitch double-knitting teaches you the structure of your fabric more thoroughly; in addition, you are working with only one color at a time, which may or may not cause a sigh of relief. The other reason to learn slip-stitch double-knitting first is that the standard method will seem like a walk in the park by comparison. I did two full-length scarves using this technique, and taught many workshops in it before I worked out the possibility of double-knitting in the currently-accepted standard method. As a matter of fact, I taught workshops using this method even after I had switched to the standard method for all my own work — for the reasons I listed above.

Unlike standard double-knitting, slip-stitch double-knitting requires an extra pair of stitches which are used on either side of the work as edge stitches. There are a couple of different ways to deal with the edges, but they both require only one extra stitch at the end (and beginning) of each row. Because of the edge stitches, you will need to add one pair to the number of pairs you're casting on for your pattern.

SLIP-STITCH DOUBLE-KNITTING CAST-ON METHOD

The slip-stitch double-knitting cast-on is similar to the standard double-knitting cast-on, in that you are working something similar to a long-tail cast-on but with one color over each finger. However, whereas the standard double-knitting cast-on is done with both ends feeding from the source yarn balls, the slip-stitch method uses a cast-on that's half sourced from one of the yarn balls and half actual long-tail. So there is some guesswork

here, as with normal long-tail. In these instructions, Color A is your lighter color and Color B is your darker color. You will need a circular or double-pointed needle — both ends of the needle are used in this technique.

1) Take Color B and make a long tail with it. No knots; just pick a point that gives you a sufficiently long tail.

2) Take Color A, with a short tail, and place it alongside Color B so that the tail points in the opposite direction. Make a slip-knot that tightens in the direction of the short tail, and put it on your needle.

3) On one side of your slip-knot, you should have a long tail of Color B and the active end of Color A; on the other side you should have a short tail of Color A and the active end of Color B.

4) Position your left hand in the same way as with the standard double-knitting cast-on, with the long tail of Color B as FC and the active end of Color A as TC.

5) Work the cast-on stitches, starting with the reverse long-tail cast-on stitch and finishing the pair with the standard long-tail cast-on stitch. You should be starting with Color A and ending with Color B. Stop when you've reached the number of pairs you need. As with the regular long-tail cast-on, if you run out of Color B, you'll need to start over with a longer tail.

6) Remove and untie the slip-knot from the beginning of the cast-on.

You will now have a cast-on with a short tail of Color B and the active end of Color A at one side of the work, and a short tail of Color A and the active end of Color B at the other.

SLIP-STITCH DOUBLE-KNITTING

The following sequence is long, but actually encompasses two rows of double-knitting.

1) Turn your work so you'll be starting with the active end of Color A.

2) Work your edge stitch (see edge stitches, below)

3) Wyib, K1; Wyif, Sl1

4) Repeat to the end of your work. Remove and untie the slip-knot. You now have both active ends at the same side of your work.

5) Turn, pick up the active end of Color B.

6) Work your edge stitch

7) Wyib, K1; Wyif, Sl1

8) Repeat to the end of your work.

9) Slide the needle back and pick up the active end of Color A.

10) Work your edge stitch

11) Wyib, Sl1; Wyif, P1

12) Repeat to the end of your work.

13) Turn, pick up the active end of Color B.

14) Work your edge stitch

15) Wyib, Sl1; Wyif, P1

16) Repeat to the end of your work.

You will notice that it each row is made up of two passes when working in only one color at a time. In the first pass, you work all the knit stitches and slip all the purls. In the second pass, you use the other color to knit all the stitches you slipped in the first pass, and slip all the stitches you knit.

This is misleading, however, since it doesn't take into account the color changes. As a matter of fact, when color-changing is in effect, you will work all the stitches that will be Color A — regardless of which side of the work they are on — and slip all the others in the first pass; in the second pass, you will work all the stitches that will be Color B, and slip all the ones you worked in the first pass.

To work a pair in the same color configuration as the background, assuming you are starting with Color A and Color A is the background, Wyib, K1; Wyif, Sl1.

To work a pair in the opposite color configuration, as-

suming the same conditions as above: Wyib, Sl1; Wyif, P1.

When returning with Color B in the other direction, you will find that the pairs worked as background will be worked the same way in Color B — knit, then slipped; likewise, those that are worked in the opposite color configuration will be worked in the same way as the instructions above for the opposite configuration, but again with Color B.

On the second row, however, things get even weirder. On the first two passes — the first complete row — you were working with Color A on the facing side and Color B on the opposite side. You went across with Color A, looking at Color A on the front, then turned and did the same with Color B. But with the second row, you will be looking at Color B while working with Color A on the opposite side:

To work a pair in the same color configuration as the background, assuming you are starting with Color A and Color B is the facing background color: Wyib, Sl1; Wyif, P1.

To work in the opposite color configuration, assuming the same conditions as above: Wyib, K1; Wyif, Sl1.

The same instructions hold for the second pass with Color B, which will again be worked while looking at Color A on the facing side.

SLIP-STITCH DOUBLE-KNITTING EDGE STITCHES

There are two edges I've used in slip-stitch double-knitting. There may be other, better ones, but this Is not a discipline I've dedicated much time to recently, so I'll document here the edges I used while I was teaching this technique.

The first edge is quick and dirty — it has a pattern to it, but it's not that nice-looking. If you don't like it, you can always do a crochet-chain edge over it to hide it afterward.

1) On the first stitch of every pass, p1

2) On the last stitch of every pass, k1

On even-numbered passes — the half-rows where you are working with Color B — you will be picking up one of two active ends that are next to each other at the beginning of the pass. You'll want to pick up Color B from underneath the Color A end when making the first edge stitch.

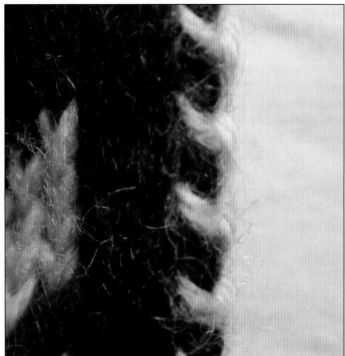

In fact, it probably doesn't matter as long as you're consistent, but I found that this direction was better than the alternative.

The second edge is much cleaner and prettier, but is more work and requires you to keep more diligent track of which pass and row you are on:

1) In pass 1, purl 1st stitch and slip last stitch with end in front

2) In pass 2, same as pass 1

3) In pass 3, slip 1st stitch with end in back, knit last stitch

4) In pass 4, same as pass 3, but be sure to take Color B from underneath Color A on the first stitch.

This edge makes it look as if the two sides were stitched together, and was, at the time I discovered it, the cleanest edge I could accomplish in slip-stitch double-knitting.

SLIP-STITCH DOUBLE-KNITTING SUMMARY

To simplify all of this, here some basic rules that you can remember to help you keep track of your work while doing slip-stitch double-knitting:

First, using DPNs or circular needles, cast-on one extra pair than you need for your pattern, starting the cast-on with Color A.

Second, the first and last stitches (not pairs) are edge stitches. All the other stitches in between are worked as pairs.

Third, there are only two types of pairs ever worked in slip-stitch double-knitting, either for opposite-side rows or for color-changing:

1)   Wyib, K1; Wyif, Sl1
2)   Wyib, Sl1; Wyif, P1

Fourth, you will always alternate the colors you are working with. You will either turn or slide your work back to the other end of your needle to access the end of the next color you need.

Fifth, if you have to set your work down and you forget which pass of a row you are on, you have done the first pass if you have both active ends at one end of the work, and you have completed the row if the active ends are at opposite ends of the work.

SLIP-STITCH DOUBLE-KNITTING DECREASES

Decreases in this type of double-knitting require the same type of preparation, but a bit more foresight. Because the fabric is worked only one color at a time, the decrease will be half-made with the first pass, and completed when the second pass is made. The decrease preparation can be done as you work the first pass; one side of the decrease itself can be done immediately with the color you are working with. The other prepared decrease stitches are to be slipped (wyib or wyif, depending on whether the decrease includes a color change) and kept together until Color B comes back and makes them back into one stitch again.

SLIP-STITCH DOUBLE-KNITTING INCREASES

These are done in much the same way as in standard double-knitting, but to keep the direction the same, a right-side increase will be followed on the opposite side with a left-side increase, and vice versa.

For an increase which is right-side on the facing side of the work, you work the increase normally into the facing stitch of the pair, then work the facing stitch itself. Slip the second stitch in the pair and continue. On the way back with Color B, you'll work the first stitch in the pair, slip the next, then bring the end to the back and work a left-side increase on the previous column. Slip the next stitch and the increase is done.

For an increase which is left-side on the facing side of the work, knit and slip the pair, then increase into the left side of the facing stitch in the pair. On the way back, work as normal up to the increased stitch. Make a right-side increase on the next column, slip the other increased stitch, and then work the next pair as normal. The increase is done.

Both of these increases assume you are on an odd-numbered row with no color changes involved in the increase. I will leave increases in even-numbered rows and color changes as an exercise to the motivated reader.

SLIP-STITCH DOUBLE-KNITTING BIND-OFF

Bind-offs are done in the same way as the bind-offs for standard double-knitting. However, because you are working the row in both directions, there is no easy way to bind off while working the row. Instead, complete the row, then bind off by slipping the stitches rather than working them. You can do this starting from either end, using either the standard or the decorative bind-off.

SLIP-STITCH DOUBLE-KNITTING IN THE ROUND

As with standard double-knitting in the round, slip-stitch double-knitting in the round eliminates the edges, so if you want to cast-on for this, use the cast-on method outlined above, but start with Color A as FC and Color B as TC — and start with a standard long-tail stitch followed by a reverse long-tail stitch. When you finish the cast-on, you will have your active ends on opposite ends of the work. Bring the end of the cast-on around the back and join with the beginning. Work the first pass with Color A as normal for slip-stitch double-knitting. Now here's where it gets interesting. When you reach the end of the first pass, both ends will be together again. Bring them both to the front of the work, then turn the work inside out and work back in the other direction with Color B. You don't, strictly speaking, have to turn the work inside-out, but I find it's easier to work the opposite side on the outside of the work than on the inside.

When you get to the end of the second pass (the first complete round), turn the work inside out again and continue with Color A — this will be the first pass of an even-numbered round. Follow that pass with a second pass in the opposite direction with Color B to complete the round.

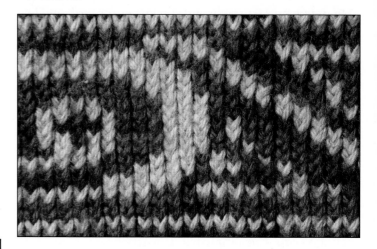

Now, think about what you are doing. The structure of this fabric is different from standard double-knitting in the round in one important way. Circular knitting in general is comprised of a long coil. At the end of the cast-on, you begin knitting on the top of the first cast-on stitch or pair. This creates the undesirable but often unavoidable effect of a jog, where the beginning and end of each round are offset by a single stitch. In slip-stitch double-knitting in the round, the coil on the facing side goes in one direction, whereas the coil on the opposite side goes in the other direction. This has the effect of pulling the jog straight. In my opinion, this is the only truly valid reason to engage in slip-stitch double-knitting in the round.

TWO-PATTERN SLIP-STITCH DOUBLE-KNITTING

As with two-pattern standard double-knitting, this requires you break some of the rules set out earlier in this section. You have learned that there are two types of pair in slip-stitch double-knitting — but in order to do two patterns, you need to add two more types of pair. For two-pattern slip-stitch double-knitting, the four types of pair are:

1) Wyib, K1; Wyif, Sl1
2) Wyib, Sl1, Wyif, P1
3) Wyib, Sl1, Wyif, Sl1
4) Wyib, K1, Wyif, P1

The other two types of pairs are there to allow you to deposit either both stitches or neither stitch in a pair in a particular color — and on the second pass, pairs that were both slipped are both worked, and pairs that were both worked are both slipped. This is a departure from the single-pattern variety, where a given pair is worked the same way on both passes.

TUBULAR 1-COLOR DOUBLE-KNITTING

This is not really a technique that is relevant to this book, but it deserves a nod since it may be the predecessor to the rest of the techniques. Ironically, despite this, it is easier to explain if you already understand the methods used to create two-color double-knitting.

Essentially, tubular double-knitting is a method you can use to create a small-diameter tube on a single pair of straight needles. It bears a resemblance to the technique of slip-stitch double-knitting, but instead of turning and sliding, you always turn — so straight needles work fine — and instead of two colors, there's only one. Because there's only one color, you need to take special care not to work a stitch you should be slipping, because you will lock the tube together. This is not as much of a problem with double-knitting done strictly for colorwork reasons — the worst that will happen is that you have a color change where there isn't supposed to be one.

Tubular double-knitting is best cast-on to a circular

needle. Use your favorite single-faced knitting cast-on — it must be an even number of stitches — then push the middle of the cast-on to the middle of the circular needle's cord and pinch the cord out from between the two stitches on either side of the midpoint. Slide the work back to the points of the circular needle — now the beginning and the end of the work are at the points, and parallel to each other. The end of the cast-on should be on the back needle.

Take another circular needle or DPN and slip the first stitch from the front needle onto it, then the first stitch from the back needle. Repeat this until all the stitches are on the new needle.

At this point, slide the work back so the active end is accessible. Take the first straight needle you plan to use for the work itself (you can, of course, use any needle — it doesn't have to be a straight), and work as if you were doing the first pass of a slip-stitch double-knitting row: Wyib, K1; Wyif, Sl1. When you reach the end of this pass, turn and repeat the same again.

After several rounds, you will notice that the object you are knitting is hollow and open at one end.

Many people who do tubular double-knitting swear by the all-purl method rather than the all-knit method. The benefit this has over the method I describe above is that the end doesn't have to be moved from side to side with every pair. Try it: set up the work the same way, but purl the first stitch, then slip the next. You'll notice that since your end is already in the front, you don't have to move the end to the front before slipping the second stitch in the pair. Of course, this gives you purl stitches on the outside — you will be working in reverse stockinette — and when the item is done you can turn it inside out to show the stockinette side.

For a more in-depth look at tubular double-knitting, find a copy of Beverly Royce's out-of-print book, or wait for the upcoming book by Kelly Klem.

QUADRUPLE KNITTING

This is one of those techniques that can be classified as something to do "because you can." There's no practical use for it as far as I can tell, but it's fun to say you can do it. It's a cross between standard double-knitting and the slip-stitch method. It'll allow you to do a standard double-knit piece in the round with only a pair of straight needles.

Begin with a circular needle, casting on an even number

of pairs using the standard double-knitting cast-on, with Color A as FC and Color B as TC. Slide the middle of the cast-on onto the cord of the circular needle and pinch the cord out between the two pairs on either side of the midpoint. Slide the work back to the points of the circular needle — similar to the slip-stitch method of preparation. The end of the cast-on should be on the back needle.

Take another circular needle or DPN and slip the first pair from the front needle, then the first pair from the back needle. Repeat this until all the pairs are on the new needle.

At this point, slide the work back so the active ends are accessible. With one of the straight needles you plan to work on, start working the first pass. With both ends in back, K1 with the color indicated by the pattern; with both ends in front, P1 with the opposite color. Slip the next pair. Repeat this until the end of the first pass. Turn and repeat.

Continue until you get tired of the technique and decide to change back to the normal method, or until you get to the decreases and it gets really impractical.

TEXTURED DOUBLE-KNITTING

Tired of doing all double-stockinette all the time? You can actually put textures onto your surfaces, if you want — but use this sparingly.

Textured double-knitting breaks two further rules — the rule that the facing stitch will always be knitted and the opposite stitch will always be purled, and the rule that the ends must travel together for the duration of the row or round.

DOUBLE-KNITTING IN REVERSE STOCKINETTE

For this entire technique, both ends will stay separate, except at the edges where they'll twist together. For ease of yarn movement, both ends will travel on the outside of the side they will be used on. They will not enter the inside of the work at all unless there is a need to make a color change.

1) Line up the ends so Color A runs along the outside of the facing side and Color B runs along the opposite side.

2) P1 Color A, K1 Color B

3) If working flat, turn, give the ends a twist

— 360 degrees if no color change is being made from the previous row, or 180 degrees if there is a color change. Line up ends to match side colors. If knitting in the round, just continue with step 2.

4) P1 Color B, K1 Color A to end of row

If you want to make a color change, cross the ends in the middle of the work so the opposite colors are lined up on the outside of the work, then work the pair as set up.

DOUBLE-KNITTING IN 1X1 RIBBING

Double-knit ribbing is a contradiction in terms. Ribbing is nice and clean to look at, but serves a function — it makes your fabric more elastic and grips the wearer's head, or wrists, or whatever, to help the garment fit better. However, double-knitting is based on 1x1 ribbing, as I mentioned way back at the beginning of the book. Adding 1x1 ribbing to surfaces created by a derivative of 1x1 ribbing really won't do anything but look silly. The fabric certainly won't compress much, especially when preceded or succeeded by cast-on, bind-off or color-changing, all of which keep the fabric from separating and the layers from operating on their own. Nevertheless, I'll show you how to do it and let you make the aesthetic faux pas if you so choose.

Despite the above opinion, I really like the rhythm of the yarn movement in this technique. It requires an even-number cast-on.

1) With both ends in back, K1 Color A.

2) Bring Color A to front. K1 Color B.

3) P1 Color A. Bring Color B to front.

4) P1 Color B. Bring both ends to the back.

5) Repeat to end. If working flat, turn, twist, and continue with steps 6-10.

6) With both ends in back, K1 Color B.

7) Bring Color B to front. K1 Color A.

8) P1 Color B. Bring Color A to front.

9) P1 Color A. Bring both ends to back.

10) Repeat to end. Turn, twist and continue with step 1.

DOUBLE-KNITTING CORRUGATED RIB

This is a 1x1 rib with color-changed purls. There are two varieties — one which has the knits and purls reversed in color on the opposite side, and one that is identical on both sides. Both require an even number of pairs cast on.

For two identical faces (identical to the photo above):

1) With both ends in back, K1 Color A.

2) Bring Color A to front. K1 Color B.

3) Bring Color B to front, Color A to back. P1 Color B.

4) P1 Color A. Bring both ends to the back.

5) Repeat 1-4 to end. If working flat, turn, give ends a twist, and repeat steps above.

For colors and stitches reversed (photo next column);

1) With both ends in back, K1 Color A.

2) With both ends in front, P1 Color B.

3) Bring Color A to back. P1 Color B.

4) K1 Color A. Bring Color B to back.

5) Repeat 1-4 to end. If working flat, turn, twist, and continue with 6-10

6) Bring Color A to front and Color B to back. P1 Color A.

7) K1 Color B. Bring Color A to back.

8) K1 Color B. Bring both ends to front.

9) P1 Color A. Bring Color B to back.

10) Repeat to end; turn, twist and continue with step 1 again.

DOUBLE-KNITTING IN SEED-STITCH

Everyone seems to think seed-stitch looks awesome. I concur — it's a great basic stitch pattern to have in your toolkit and easy to do in double-knitting as well. Since double-knitting already holds itself flat, there's no need to use seed-stitch for the same purpose, but it still has design potential and holds gauge well. There are two methods. For seed-stitch in flat double-knitting, cast on an even number of pairs.

1) With both ends in back, K1 Color A

2) Bring Color A to front. K1 Color B.

3) P1 Color A. Bring Color A to front.

4) P1 Color B. Bring both ends to back.
5) Repeat to end. If working flat, turn, twist, and follow steps 6-10.

6) Bring Color B to the front and Color A to the back. P1 Color B.

7) Bring Color A to front. P1 Color A.

8) Bring both ends to the back. K1 Color B.

9) Bring Color B to front. K1 Color A.

10) Repeat from 6-9 to end. Turn, twist and continue with step 1.

If working circularly, when you come to the end of the round, because there are an even number of steps and an odd number of pairs, you will be following steps 1 and 2 again. Just continue with steps 3 and 4 as you begin the next round, and you'll never notice the jog.

CHECKERBOARD SEED-STITCH

Let's combine seed-stitch with corrugated rib and see what happens! Like corrugated rib, you can do checkerboard seed-stitch in one of two ways. In either case, there's no reason to twist at the edges because every pair is a color change from the one below (not to mention the other three around it). Like solid-colored seed-stitch, you'll need to cast on an even number of pairs for flat work, or an odd number for circular work.

Both sides identical (identical to the photo above):

1) With both ends in back, K1 Color A.

2) Bring Color A to front. K1 Color B.

3) Bring Color B to front, Color A to back. P1 Color B.

4) Bring Color A to front. P1 Color A.

5) Repeat to end. If working flat, turn and continue with steps 6-10.

6) Bring Color B to front, Color A to back. P1 Color B.

7) Bring Color A to front, P1 Color A.

8) Bring both ends to back. K1 Color A.

9) Bring Color A to front, K1 Color B.

10) Repeat 6-9 to end. Turn, start over from 1.

Opposite colors on either side (below):

1) With both ends in back, K1 Color A.

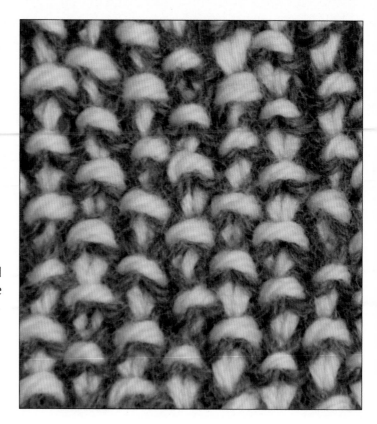

2) With both ends in front, P1 Color B.

3) Bring Color A to back. P1 Color B

4) K1 Color A. Bring Color B to back.

5) Repeat to end. If working flat, turn and continue with steps 6-10

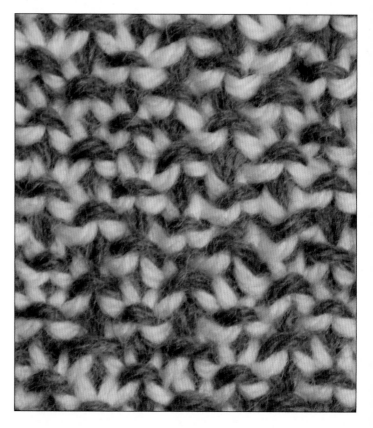

6) With both ends in back, K1 Color B.

7) With both ends in front, P1 Color A.

8) Bring Color B to back. P1 Color A.

9) K1 Color B. Bring Color A to back.

10) Repeat 6-9 to end. Turn, start over from 1.

DOUBLE-KNITTING BASIC OPENWORK

This is a technique I wasn't sure I wanted to include in the book, but the fabric is just so interesting that I couldn't leave it out completely. I am usually against techniques that diverge so much from the rules of double-knitting that they can't really be called double-knitting any more. This technique is really close to that line, but the fabric has some interesting properties that I really feel need to see the light of day.

Probably the simplest openwork stitch pattern is the well-known "K2Tog, yo" which can be repeated aligned or offset to create columns or diagonal stripes of holes in your knitting. I've accomplished the same in double-knitting with relatively little modification — and an interesting and unexpected side-effect: the two layers are locked together due to the interaction of the yarn-overs.

And even better, they're locked together a half-pair off from each other, which means that rather than showing holes all the way through the work, each hole generated by a yarn-over has a solid background behind it, on both sides.

Some caveats about this technique: first, don't try to do a selvedge with it. Doing a yarn-over next to a selvedge becomes really messy when both ends are brought to the front. Instead, the two pairs at the edges are always worked in both directions, as with the standard closed double-knit edge. Because these pairs are always worked, they are kept separate from the pattern and are never incorporated into a decrease. You could even switch their color configuration if you wanted to be dramatic about it.

Second, the reason I said this technique diverges a little too much from the technique of double-knitting is that the number of decreases required means that every pair (other than the edge pairs) will be separated and reordered at some point during every odd-numbered row. The act of separating the layers so completely means that the technique departs from double-knitting — but the layers are separated only temporarily and only two pairs at a time, so we're not over the edge quite yet.

Third, rather than using the more traditional K2Tog, I use SSK in this pattern. You can certainly use K2Tog if you prefer, but remember that you have to follow it up with an SSP, which is an annoying stitch to do so many times in every row.

Fourth, when doing a yarn-over, do so with both ends held together. Keep the two ends in the correct orientation while you do it. They should not twist, and the resulting pair should be Color A, then Color B. If they

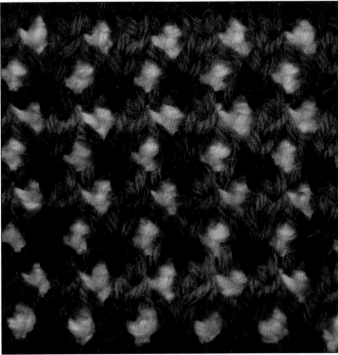

switch places between this row and the next, they should be easily reordered as long as the order they were originally placed in was correct.

Now, on to the pattern.

First, cast on an even number of pairs, using Color A as TC and Color B as FC. Turn and begin with two plain rows. If you'd prefer to start the openwork closer to the cast-on, you can use Color A as FC and Color B as TC, and work one plain row before starting. But I don't recommend starting the openwork directly off the cast-on. It can be done but reordering the stitches on such a tight row is difficult.

1) Work 1 pair as normal

2) (Left-slanting decrease, yarn-over) until 1 pair is left on the needle.

3) Work 1 pair as normal.

4) Turn, twist, work across as normal in matching colors. Be careful to keep the YOs from hopping forward over the preceding pairs and getting worked before their time.

5) Turn, work 1 pair as normal

6) (Yarn-over, left-slanting decrease) until 1 pair is left on the needle.

7) Work 1 pair as normal.

8) Repeat step 4. Turn.

It should be theoretically possible to do other, more complex openwork in double-knitting. I will leave that experimentation up to you!

DOUBLE-KNITTING SHORT ROWS

Short rows are all about the "wrap and turn" move that allows you to start working back in the other direction in the middle of a row without leaving a hole. There are other resources for in-depth short row exploration, but the basic move involves wrapping the yarn around the next stitch to anchor it, then turning your work as if you were at the end of a row. The challenge with double-knitting is that the technique must be done in a fashion which will keep the two layers separate if necessary. One of the primary uses of short-rows in everyday knitting is for sock heels. One of the classic uses of double-knitting

is to make two socks, one inside the other. If you lock the socks together by switching sides by mistake, or by using a technique that doesn't keep the sides separate, you've defeated the purpose of the double-sock trick. I'm not going to go into the two socks pattern here; it's available on Knitty.com if you're interested.

It's the wrap that poses the difficulty — the two ends must be wrapped separately around the bases of the two stitches comprising the next pair. I've seen short-row wraps from back to front and from front to back — the only difference seems to be similar to the difference between twisted and untwisted stitches, except that you're not using many of them next to each other to create a fabric. In double-knitting, the temptation is to wrap from inside (where the strands already live) to outside, but I find the opposite is better.

Because the end has to start its next row on the inside, it's best to put it where it wants to be.

First, work to the end of the short row. The next pair will be wrapped around, and the pair you just finished will be the beginning of the next short row.

To wrap from outside to inside, as recommended:

1) Bring Color A forward. Slip 2.

2) Bring Color B forward. Pass 1 back.

3) Bring both ends to back. Pass 1 back.

4) Turn, and start your next row.

To wrap from inside to outside:

1) With both ends in back, slip 1.

2) With both ends in front, slip 1.

3) Bring Color B to the back. Pass 2 back.

4) Turn, and start your next row.

ALTERNATIVE DOUBLE-KNITTING DECREASES

I do not have illustrations for these elegant methods for the two single-decrease types. They are a relatively recent discovery, first posited to me by Suzanne Ress, one of my students and subsequently a sample knitter for two of my published patterns. I have refined them a little and integrated them into two decreases. I have not found an equally elegant method to use similar techniques on the double-decrease setup.

These decreases don't require the reordering of stitches to set up the pairs — that is taken care of in the technique itself. The outcome of both is identical to the outcome of the corresponding decrease illustrated earlier in the book.

RIGHT-SLANTING DECREASE

1) Work up to the first pair to be included in the decrease.

2) Slip first stitch purlwise

3) Slip next two stitches together knitwise.

4) Slip last stitch knitwise.

5) Pass 2 back to left needle.

6) Insert left needle through the first stitch on the right needle, in the same orientation as the right needle tip. Return this loop to the left needle. I call this a "Pass back untwisted."

7) Pass 1 back to left needle.

8) K2Tog.

9) P2TogTBL.

LEFT-SLANTING DECREASE

1) Work up to the first pair to be included in the decrease.

2) Slip first stitch knitwise

3) Slip next two stitches together knitwise

4) Pass 1 back untwisted.

5) You have now reordered your pairs. The two knits are both twisted and the purls are not. Insert your left needle into the two knit stitches on the right needle from the front.

6) Complete the SSK by wrapping the end of the color required by the pattern.

7) P2Tog the next 2 stitches on the left needle.

DOUBLE-DECREASE SETUP

There is a way to do this, but it's sort of like those "Tower of Hanoi" puzzles. I feel like the method is overly labor-intensive but if you want to try it, it will at least keep you from having to drop and pick up free loops.

1) Work up to the first pair to be included in the double-decrease.

2) Slip first stitch purlwise.

3) Slip next two stitches together knitwise.

4) Slip next two stitches together knitwise.

5) Pass 3 separately back untwisted.

6) Slip next two stitches together knitwise.

7) Pass 3 separately back untwisted.

8) Pass 1 back to left needle.

At this point you are set up for either double-decrease as laid out in the chapter on Shaping (page 54).

GLOBAL KEY OF CHART ELEMENTS

Note: When working on the opposite side, chart elements that are orientable reverse direction. "Knit" becomes "purl"; "right" becomes "left" and "facing" becomes "opposite".

\	Left-slanting Decrease
/	Right-slanting Decrease
∧	Standard Double-Decrease
人	Ridged Double-Decrease
⋀	Double-Decrease/Left-side Increase
V	Right-side Increase
⅄	Left-side Increase
∨	Double-Increase
⨉	Shift left
•	Purl
⬎ \	Two-pattern Left-slanting Decrease
⬏ /	Two-pattern Right-slanting Decrease
⨳	2p2 (Lock Purl)
⨝	2k2 (Lock Knit)
⟩⟨	C3F (Cable 3 Front)
⟩⟨	C3B (Cable 3 Back)
⟩ ⟨	C2Under3
⟩⟨	C2Over3
⟩⟨	C2F (Cable 2 Front)
⟩⟨	C2B (Cable 2 Back)
⟩ ⟨	C1Under2
⟩⟨	C1Over2
⟩⟨	C1F
⟩⟨	C1B
⟩⟨	C1FDec
◖	Selvedge on facing side
◗	Selvedge on opposite side

188

GLOSSARY OF ABBREVIATIONS

DPN	Double-pointed needle
K	Knit
P	Purl
Sl	Slip (purlwise unless specified)
Wyib	"With yarn in back" — with all ends in back
Wyif	"With yarn in front" — with all ends in front
TC	Thumb Color: the color of the end over your thumb while casting on.
FC	Finger Color: the color of the end over your finger while casting on.
K2Tog	Knit 2 together
P2Tog	Purl 2 together
K2TogTBL	Knit 2 together through the back loop
P2TogTBL	Purl 2 together through the back loop
SSK	Slip slip knit
SSP	Slip slip purl
PSSO	Pass second stitch over (the first stitch and off the needle)
PTSO	Pass third stitch over (the first and second stitches and off the needle)
P2SO	Pass 2 stitches over (the first stitch and off the needle)
2K2	K2tog with both ends held together
2P2	P2tog with both ends held together
2K2Tog	K4tog with both ends held together
2P2Tog	P4tog with both ends held together
2P3Tog	P6tog with both ends held together
CxB	Where "x" is a number of pairs — a symmetrical cable where the cable needle is held to the back
CxF	Where "x" is a number of pairs — a symmetrical cable where the cable needle is held to the front.
CxUNDERy	Where "x" and "y" are different numbers of pairs — an asymmetrical cable where the cable needle is held to the back with "x" pairs.
CxOVERy	Where "x" and "y" are different numbers of pairs — an asymmetrical cable where the cable needle is held to the front with "x" pairs.
C1FDec	A three-pair combination single cross cable and decrease (see page 126)

GLOSSARY OF TERMS

Front	The front side of the work as you are looking at it at any given time.
Back	The back side of the work as you are looking at it at any given time.
Facing (side)	The front of the work as denoted by the pattern.
Opposite (side)	The back of the work, usually not charted, as denoted by the pattern.
Pair	What double-knitting has instead of "stitch" — two stitches on opposite sides of the work, always worked in concert with each other.
Double-stockinette	The typical double-knitted fabric which looks like two layers of stockinette, back to back.
Plain double-stockinette	The typical double-knitted fabric as above, but assuming two colors and no color changes. Plain double-stockinette is hollow.
Orientation	A stitch's position on the needle, resulting in a twisted or untwisted stitch.
Configuration	The order of colors in a pair.
Reorder	To separate a sequence of pairs into groupings of knit and purl stitches, typically in preparation for decreasing.
Pass back	A slip in the opposite direction, always purlwise (incorporating no twist).
Pass back untwisted	A slip in the opposite direction that untwists a knitwise slip so the passed stitch is in the original orientation again.
End(s)	Short for "active end(s)": the yarn(s) you are working with.
Strand	The yarn you have already worked with, which is now part of your fabric.
Pixel	A colored square on a chart, used in concert with other pixels of other colors to create a picture.
Chart element	An icon on a chart that indicates a type of stitch or combination of stitches.

ACKNOWLEDGEMENTS

In addition to those to whom I dedicated the book, I'd like to thank the following people:

My family, for lending moral support to my most recent obsession.

Cat Bordhi, for running the Visionary Retreat in 2010 which got me moving for real, and the other Visionaries for their constructive criticism and words of wisdom.

Shannon Okey, for seeing the promise in my work before I'd even pitched the book to other publishers.

Julia Farwell-Clay, for giving me a first opportunity to publish in Twist Collective (http://www.twistcollective.com)

Jessica Tromp, for letting me use one of the charts she's published on http://www.jessica-tromp.nl

Kieran Foley, for the inspiration to move my colorwork off the grid, at http://www.kieranfoley.com

Lucy Lee, for helping me develop the predecessor to my double-knit cast-on, and for everything else she does for the Cambridge knitting community from her base at http://www.mindseyeyarns.com

Julie Levy, for the red-pen treatment.

Berroco, Cascade, Crystal Palace and Webs for their gracious yarn assistance

And to my wonderful sample knitters, without whose help I would not have been able to finish knitting before I had to write the text:

Beth Levine (Beth02116 on Ravelry) from MA
Stacey Trock (www.freshstitches.com/wordpress) from CT
Astra from MA
Shelley Winiger from ND
Marialyce Weideman (marimariknit on Ravelry) from NV
Radka Chamberlain (radka-knits.blogspot.com) from PA
Michelle Gibbs (theboringknitter.com) from ME by way of MA
Suzanne Ress (owlknits.blogspot.com) from MA

BIBLIOGRAPHY

These are works that deal primarily with double-knitting or include some double-knitting instructions while focusing on reversible knitting.

- Royce, Beverly. Notes on Double Knitting. Pittsville, WI: Schoolhouse, 1994. Print.
- Neighbors, Jane. Reversible Two-color Knitting. New York: Scribner, 1974. Print.
- Neatby, Lucy. Double Knitting Delight 1. Nova Scotia: Tradewind Knitwear Designs, 2007. DVD.
- Baber, M'Lou. Double Knitting: Reversible Two-color Designs. Pittsville, WI: Schoolhouse, 2008. Print.
- Schreier, Iris. Iris Schreier's Reversible Knits: Creative Techniques for Knitting Both Sides Right. New York, NY: Lark, 2009. Print.
- Barr, Lynne. Reversible Knitting: 50 Brand-new, Groundbreaking Stitch Patterns. New York: Stewart, Tabori & Chang, 2009. Print.

These are my favorite two-color chart books which are ideal for use in double-knitting patterns:

- Starmore, Alice. Charts for Colour Knitting. Achmore, Isle of Lewis, Scotland: Windfall, 1992. Print.
- Spinhoven, Co. Celtic Charted Designs. New York: Dover Publications, 1987. Print.
- Spies, Nancy. Here Be Wyverns: Hundreds of Patterns Graphed from Medieval Sources. Jarretsville, MD: Arelate Studio, 2002. Print.
- Cartwright-Jones, Catherine, and Roy Jones. Enchanted Knitting: Charted Motifs for Hand and Machine Knitting. Loveland, CO: Interweave, 1997. Print.
- Cartwright-Jones, Catherine, and Roy Jones. The Tap-Dancing Lizard: 337 Fanciful Charts for the Adventurous Knitter. Loveland, CO: Interweave, 1992. Print.
- Harrell, Betsy. Anatolian Knitting Designs: Sivas Stocking Patterns Collected in an Istanbul Shantytown. Istanbul: Redhouse, 1981. Print.

These are books that were mentioned in the text and don't have anything directly to do with double-knitting but that you may find helpful.

- Galeskas, Bev. The Magic Loop: Working around on One Needle. East Wenatchee, WA: Fiber Trends, 2002. Print.
- Bordhi, Cat. Socks Soar on Two Circular Needles: a Manual of Elegant Knitting Techniques and Patterns. Friday Harbor, WA: Passing Paws, 2001. Print.

ABOUT ALASDAIR

Alasdair Post-Quinn grew up in Vermont. He has been crafting since age 4, teaching crafts since age 12, knitting since age 26, double-knitting since age 27, teaching double-knitting since age 28, and thinking about writing a book on double-knitting since age 29. He is now 34 and lives in Cambridge, MA, with his wife and cat. In his time outside of knitting, he fixes computers for Brandeis University, enjoys cooking and eating good food, listens to esoteric music, audiobooks, and NPR, and tries to spend as much time outdoors as possible.

Visit Alasdair online, or in his Ravelry group Fallingblox Designs.

double-knitting.com

ABOUT COOPERATIVE PRESS
partners in publishing

Cooperative Press (formerly anezka media) was founded in 2007 by Shannon Okey, a voracious reader as well as writer and editor, who had been doing freelance acquisitions work, introducing authors with projects she believed in to editors at various publishers.

Although working with traditional publishers can be very rewarding, there are some books that fly under their radar. They're too avant-garde, or the marketing department doesn't know how to sell them, or they don't think they'll sell 50,000 copies in a year.

5,000 or 50,000. Does the book matter to that 5,000? Then it should be published.

In 2009, Cooperative Press changed its named to reflect the relationships we have developed with authors working on books. We work together to put out the best quality books we can and share in the proceeds accordingly.

Thank you for supporting independent publishers and authors.

Join our mailing list for information on upcoming books!

cooperativepress.com